PRAISE FOR CECILIA KONCHAR FARR

"The author provides her readers with a new set of guidelines for judging literary works, specifically novels . . . *The Ulysses Delusion* is an ideal model of clear, thoughtful, balanced, witty, and well-written criticism—something I find in extremely short supply these days . . . Konchar Farr's own writing succeeds admirably. This book really is a page-turner."

—Mallory Young, *TSWL Tulsa Studies in Women's Literature*, Vol. 38 (2), (2019)

"*The Ulysses Delusion* is an engaging discussion of the contemporary literary marketplace and the tastemakers who have framed discussions of literary quality and served as the gatekeepers to popular success in the late twentieth and early twenty-first centuries. Konchar Farr's unapologetic championing of the accessible is both ideologically resonant with her thesis and admirable—she has truly produced a popular literary criticism that is both rigorous and readable."

—Amy L. Blair, Associate Professor of English at Marquette University

OTHER BOOKS AVAILABLE BY CECILIA KONCHAR FARR

The Ulysses Delusion

Reading Oprah

"AS I WAS SAYING"

A COMPANION TO GERTRUDE STEIN'S

THE MAKING OF AMERICANS

By
Cecilia Konchar Farr & Janie Sisson

DALKEY ARCHIVE PRESS
Dallas, TX / Rochester, NY

Deep Vellum | Dalkey Archive Press
3000 Commerce Street, Dallas, Texas 75226
www.dalkeyarchive.com

Deep Vellum is a 501c3 nonprofit literary arts organization founded in 2013 with the mission to bring the world into conversation through literature.

First edition, 2025

Support for this publication has been provided in part by grants from the Texas Commission on the Arts, the City of Dallas Office of Arts and Culture, and the Addy Foundation.

THE ADDY
FOUNDATION

Library of Congress Cataloging-in-Publication Data

Names: Farr, Cecilia Konchar, 1958- author | Sisson, Janie author
Title: As I was saying : a companion to Gertrude Stein's The Making of Americans /
by Cecilia Konchar Farr & Janie Sisson.
Description: Dallas, TX : Dalkey Archive Press, 2025. | Includes bibliographical references.
Identifiers: LCCN 2025039798 (print) | LCCN 2025039799 (ebook) |
ISBN 9781628974584 trade paperback | ISBN 9781628974850 ebook
Subjects: LCSH: Stein, Gertrude, 1874-1946. Making of Americans | LCGFT: Literary criticism
Classification: LCC PS3537.T323 M334 2025 (print) |
LCC PS3537.T323 (ebook) | DDC 813/.52--dc23/eng/20250904
LC record available at https://lccn.loc.gov/2025039798
LC ebook record available at https://lccn.loc.gov/2025039799

Cover art and design by Kit Schluter
Interior design and typeset by Douglas Suttle

Printed in the United States of America

"AS I WAS SAYING"

Table of Contents

Part One: *Introduction*

Part Two: *Reading the Novel*

Part Three: *Summary*

"I could though be so wise and am so wise and it would be so nice for me to be certain that from me some other one could be a wise one a little less wise than I am who am the original wise one"

The Making of Americans

"She, well she, she had written a lovely book but nobody took the lovely book nobody paid her money for the lovely book they never gave her money, never never never and she was poor and they needed money oh yes they did she and her lover."

Ida, A Novel

Part One:
Introduction

The Long Unmaking of *The Making of Americans*: Gertrude Stein and the Modernist Novel
by Cecilia Konchar Farr

THIS READING COMPANION has been a long time coming. While Gertrude Stein's *The Making of Americans* is not the first modernist experimental novel to make readers reach for a road map to chart their way through it, it's definitely challenging. Full of recurring repetitions, page-long sentences, complicated passages rooted in the psychology of personality, inexplicable narrative incursions, newly sprouted branches of the characters' family tree, detours into the lives of their maids and acquaintances—and did I mention repetition? After about 150 pages the going gets really tough when the storyline suffers a nearly complete breakdown of plot. The narrator makes us surrender Julia Dehning's romance narrative, that most familiar of structures in the history of the novel. After that, there is very little "happily ever after" or even "and then what happened." Nothing happens, and, of course, everything does—marriages and deaths, scandals and alliances, relocations, dislocations, and disclosures, all the stuff of "a decent family's progress." At every turn, this frustrating text thwarts even a practiced reader's expectations about novel reading. Some scholars won't even call it a novel. Add to this the narrator (him or herself) asserting their presence with what becomes an almost constant refrain of "As I was saying," until, in the end, everyone in "the family . . . has come to be a dead one" (829). That's a pretty definitive conclusion (and kind of a spoiler).

After years of stops and starts, frustrations and failed attempts, the one thing that finally got me all the way through *The Making of Americans* (without becoming a dead one) was having companions along for the undertaking. A professor of American literature in an undergraduate women's college, I assigned the novel for my senior seminar, and week after week seven students and I met our page goals, offered up tentative interpretations, made crazy connections, charts, and illustrations, and worked our way through to page 925. When the semester was over we realized two things: 1) Our work had paid off. Together, we had developed strategies for our reading and insights into Stein's project and its purposes. 2) We had done this with very little help, no SparkNotes, no CliffsNotes, no book called "A Companion to Gertrude Stein's *The Making of Americans*." Nevertheless, we had done it. We read the book (and made T-shirts to prove it).

But as a feminist theorist, I was truly taken aback at the difference in available resources for Stein's novel and for James Joyce's equally demanding and consciously avant-garde *Ulysses*. I had assigned *Ulysses* in a previous course, and its prominence among twentieth-century novels was the jumping off point of my study *The Ulysses Delusion*, where I work to recalibrate our standards of literary merit by more democratic measures. Both texts are avatars of the revolutionary genre-bending spirit of early twentieth-century art and literature. Both influenced the writers who followed them. So why have modernist scholars, even in this age of retheorizing, largely ignored Stein's playful and profound experimentations with the novel while celebrating Joyce's innovations? Guides to *Ulysses*—geographical, literary, illustrated, ambulatory, historical, pedagogical, theological, mythological, topographical—fill four screens on an Amazon search and cover several shelves in the PR6000 section of our library. Now type "How to read Gertrude Stein's *The Making of Americans*" into Google or your library's website and see what comes up.[1]

1. What does come up in a search deep into Google and CLICnet is a review by Michael Kaufman of George B. Moore's 1998 study, *Gertrude Stein's* The Making of Americans: *Repetition and the Emergence of Modernism*, which aims, among other things, to be a guide to reading the novel. The review begins: "In *Axel's Castle* (1931), the earliest critical assessment of Gertrude

Written by the woman who most defined "modern" for her generation, *The Making of Americans* (*TMOA*) stands as the first of its kind, the earliest overtly modernist novel. The modernist period is generally centered "between the wars," beginning around 1914 and ending about 1946, with some of its most definitive works published in the 1920s. This novel came earlier. Composed mainly between 1906 and 1908 in Paris, its context was Stein's exploration, as an expatriate, of what it meant to be American, "a real American, one whose tradition it has taken scarcely sixty years to create" (*TMOA* 3). It also sprang from her determined inquiry into what a new century could offer in psychology, art, and literature, inspired by her graduate research in neurology, her curiosity about modern painting, and her discussions with Pablo Picasso, her brother Leo, and other expatriate artists and thinkers. Widely circulated, revised, polished, and serialized before its first full publication in 1925, *TMOA* was Stein's beloved "Long Book," the one she called "the beginning, really the beginning of modern writing," the one she never stopped talking about even as she published many shorter pieces that earned her more recognition and, to this day, more scholarly attention.[2]

TMOA influenced Ernest Hemingway's style in *The Sun Also Rises*, his successful and famously modernist first novel, published in 1926, four years after he arrived, late, to the Paris expatriate scene. Stein's novel showed up at Hogarth Press, where Virginia Woolf read, commented

Stein's self-proclaimed masterpiece, *The Making of Americans*, Edmund Wilson wrote, 'I confess that I have not read this book all through, and I do not know whether it is possible to do so.'" Kaufman's assertion that this assessment is "long overdue" indicates, to him, "that we still excuse the neglect of Stein's masterwork. Unfortunately [he adds], Moore's book is unlikely to excite much new interest." Like many critics, Kaufman (with Moore) follows the practice of damning with faint praise. And he was, sadly, correct—Moore's erudite book didn't excite new interest, nor did it inhibit the neglect of Stein.

2. While (in February 2018) the *MLA International Bibliography* listed 1,522 entries under "Gertrude Stein" since 1950 (journal articles, books, book chapters, dissertations), only 72 referenced *TMOA*; by far the majority of those have been published in the last ten years.

on, and rejected it early in 1925, even while acknowledging its influence on her evolving modernist style, the style that surfaced definitively in the Stein-like sentences of her 1925 novel *Mrs. Dalloway* and increasingly in her subsequent novels, *To the Lighthouse* and *The Waves* (DuPlessis 43). *TMOA* was completed and circulated seven years before pieces of James Joyce's *Ulysses* appeared in literary magazines and eleven years before Sylvia Beach published the completed version for him in 1922. The first in Marcel Proust's series of modernist autobiographical novels saw its initial English translation that same year. William Faulkner's *The Sound and the Fury* came out in 1929.

And while there are guides to reading Joyce's, Proust's, and Faulkner's experimental novels, there is hardly a resource available for getting through Stein's.

Why is that?

I teach a three-week study abroad course in Paris every year, during my Midwestern college's J-term. On one of those visits, I attended an exhibition called "La Famille Stein," at the Grand Palais. Wandering through the reconstructions of the Stein family's modern art collections, I was captivated by Gertrude's adventurousness. The three siblings, Leo, Gertrude, and Michael, developed similar interests in art soon after they moved to Paris at the turn of the twentieth century, collecting mainly Matisse, Picasso, and Cézanne. So compelling was the experimental work of these artists that the middle-class Steins used most of their spending money to buy up their paintings. The peculiar Americans quickly became notorious for embracing what was to become a new movement in art. In fact, critics have called their collection "the first museum of modern art" (Mellow 117).

But as the modernist movement became increasingly unconventional and defiant, and as the exhibition continued chronologically—past the Fauvres, beyond the Blue period, through Cubism, Futurism, Dadaism, Surrealism and beyond—soon only Gertrude remained a collector. The final room of the exhibition spoke volumes: it was the size of an elementary school gymnasium and full of artistic renditions of Gertrude Stein. There was the famous hunched profile of the Buddha-like Jo Davidson sculpture, the masked face of the enigmatic Picasso portrait, the lightness and humor of the colorful Picabia paintings. The self-possession, the handsome heft of Gertrude Stein that I recognized from my study of the American expatriates surrounded me in paintings more numerous than I had expected, by artists I never knew had taken her as a subject. As the exhibition catalogue notes, for modernist artists "It became almost obligatory . . . to paint Gertrude Stein" (Loth).

Here was overwhelming evidence of the influence Stein had over the modernist movement in its heyday in the first half of the twentieth century. As Stein's contemporary Janet Flanner wrote in her *New Yorker* column late in the 1920s, "No American writer is taken more seriously than Miss Stein by the Paris modernists" (9). In his "Introduction" to Stein's 1922 *Geography and Plays*, writer Sherwood Anderson, too, confirmed her preeminence among the modernists, remarking on her powerful mind and "discrimination in the arts such as I have found in no other American born man or woman" (6).

Here also was visual affirmation of Stein's commitment to an idea she learned from William James when he was her teacher in college and her mentor after: "He said, 'Never reject anything. Nothing has been proved. If you reject anything, that is the beginning of the end as an intellectual,'" she recalled (Evans 143). Intellectual to the end, Stein's hungry mind followed every aesthetic trend, considered each new idea. And before critics had conceived of a modernist novel, she claimed to be redefining fiction as Picasso and Matisse were redefining visual art.

I knew as soon as I visited that exhibition that my ongoing study of the American novel was going to have to run through *TMOA*. I wondered how I could have skipped past such a significant voice from the era that engages me most as a scholar. So, I did what we do at liberal arts colleges like mine—I paired my questions with my teaching and constructed that senior seminar that would take *TMOA* as its focus. I assigned Stein's "impenetrable" novel; and then those seven English majors and I spent the next ten weeks wrestling with it. I'm not exaggerating when I say it is the most difficult book I have ever read—and, it turns out, one of the most rewarding. More on that to come.

THE LESBIAN IN THE GARDEN

So why might a Jewish lesbian's primary contribution to modernism, so clearly foundational to the movement, be overlooked or diminished across the course of the twentieth century? Why today, in fifteen screens of basic definition of modernism on *Wikipedia*, does her name not appear once? Anyone?[3]

Here it seems the most accurate answer may be the simple, obvious one. Despite the trend across my academic life for scholars to push against an elitist definition of high modernism that leaves many (nonwhite and nonmale) writers marginalized, we still fall short of embracing the centrality of this most influential of modernists.[4] Most readers are more familiar with Gertrude Stein as a cultural icon than as a writer. The legend accentuates the famous expatriate who claimed Paris as her hometown; she walked her poodle, Basket, through the Luxembourg Gardens, lived openly with her wife, Alice B. Toklas, and considered herself a genius, the equal of any man. She spurned the company of the wives of famous men, and mentored the ultra-masculine Hemingway and Picasso. Gender nonconforming, she cut her hair short and wrote impenetrable poetry and prose.

Impenetrable. That's the word I have encountered most often to describe Stein's writing.

Her reputation, the extent of her literary and cultural influence, has suffered because of homophobia and anti-Semitism. She has become legendary, "the most famous lesbian in the world" (GayHeroes.com), and

3. "Today" being March 2018

4. A lot of ink has gone into redefining American modernism over the past forty years, led by African-American and feminist scholars who have expanded its terms to include Harlem Renaissance writing, middlebrow, and genre novels, and other works by people of color and white women. Even while steering the movement away from definitions founded on the triumvirate of Faulkner-Fitzgerald-Hemingway, many critics still characterize modernism via traditional aesthetic concerns. See *Bad Modernisms* for further discussion of contemporary reconfigurations and redefinitions. Gerald Graff's *Professing Literature* also offers helpful insight into trends in literary study.

So Famous and So Gay (in Jeff Solomon's book), and her work gets crushed under the burden of the label. Her life has been reduced, through constant repetition, to inaccurate stereotypes; she is both ridiculous and delphic. The result: her face can be found on mugs and t-shirts; enigmatic quotes appear in memes and on posters, but scholars have yet to plumb the depths of her influence on the most significant aesthetic movement of the twentieth century. Absurdly, she is still sidelined to Hemingway as an innovator of American modernism, bumped by Joyce as the writer who transformed the novel, and edged out of the Anglo-American literary canon by Woolf, a WASPier, more fragile and self-effacing (and not quite so gay) woman writer.

Stein did foster friendships with artistic men—Picasso, Juan Gris, Hemingway, George Antheil, Paul Robeson, Virgil Thompson—but she also cultivated long-term relationships with many women—Dr. Claribel Cone, Natalie Clifford Barney, Sylvia Beach, Marie Laurencin, and Janet Flanner, for example. She and Toklas, who lived together as a committed couple for thirty-six years, loved to entertain; they both enjoyed good food and were generous with wine and desserts (not just those famous pot brownies). Leading modernist scholar Linda Wagner-Martin points out in her authoritative biography that only with unfamiliar guests did Toklas separate the "wives" from the "artists"; more often, Stein and Toklas preferred to sit together, to entertain both women and men; many "were welcomed enthusiastically as couples" (154). But that does not fit the legend.

What strikes me most about Stein stories is that so many of them mention her hearty laugh, "the easiest, most infectious laugh . . . that would fill the room" (Cody 74). Casual visitors and friends alike were drawn to her resonant voice, to the way she relished good ideas; she was, as Sherwood Anderson described her, "a charmingly brilliant conversationalist." As Wagner-Martin concludes, "Stein at home was difficult to resist, and it was a tribute to both her intelligence and Toklas's entrepreneurial skill that they understood how powerful she was in her own setting" (158). In her salon, Gertrude talked "with the greatest sense, coherency, simplicity, and precision," Janet Flanner remembered (155). Throughout the 1920s, Gertrude and Alice's home at 27 rue de Fleurus overflowed with company and conviviality, the center of expatriate modernism. This description couldn't veer more pointedly from the famously incomprehensible eccentric of modernist lore, the overbearing schoolmarm of Woody Allen's *Midnight in Paris*, the vindictive scold of Hemingway's *A Moveable Feast*, or other points of reference in American popular culture too numerous to name.

But what was American literary culture to do with this large woman writer, a scintillating force of nature who understood her own worth and confidently claimed her place in literary history? Stein often had difficulty finding publishers for her linguistic experiments, even as her name became one of the most recognizable in U.S. culture, even as she earned respect for her unerring assessments of contemporary art. While many young writers and editors admired her and sought her advice, they were also quick to dismiss or even make fun of her—the size of her breasts, the style of her clothes, her relationship with Alice, that cursed impenetrability. Woolf and others remarked revealingly on how Jewish she appeared, how unpolished.[5]

It may help to revisit her moment in U.S. history, the early twentieth century, when our most prestigious colleges and universities did not yet admit women and often put caps on the number of Jewish students they would accept. In the years before World War II, Jewish characters such as Fitzgerald's Meyer Wolfsheim and Hemingway's Robert Cohn were smarmy antagonists in American novels, foreshadowing Western cultural complicity in the coming Holocaust. It was a time when gender nonconformity was considered deviant, when Radclyffe Hall's *Well of Loneliness*, called the first lesbian novel, was condemned in the British courts for obscenity, despite its Victorian tone and lack of sexually explicit scenes, in a field of modernist novels seething with sexuality. Prohibition was in full

5. After Stein's visit to London, Woolf wrote about how difficult she found her, criticizing Stein's attitude, in particular. Stein "insists that she is not only the most intelligible, but also the most popular of living writers," Woolf wrote, then concluded that "Leonard, being a Jew himself, got on very well with her. But it was an anxious, exacerbating affair" (Wagner-Martin 184).

force; the doors of Ellis Island were closing for immigrants; membership in the Ku Klux Klan was growing, and women had just won the vote.

Add to all this the fact that the modernist movement in literature was defined for study in American universities when it was over, at midcentury, and mainly by the influential Southern Agrarians and the New Critics, whose theories were culturally and politically conservative, sometimes openly racist and misogynist.[6] Few white women writers, Jewish writers, or writers of color earned their attention, even as they promoted difficult modernist texts. Their celebrated triumvirate of Faulkner-Fitzgerald-Hemingway was still in ascendancy when I began studying the modernist novel in the 1980s. It took until graduate school for me to find Zora Neale Hurston, Henry Roth, Willa Cather, Anzia Yezierska, Nella Larsen, or Langston Hughes (whose account of expatriate Parisian shenanigans in *The Big Sea* is still my favorite). So when critics constructed American modernism after the fact, there was space for the mythic Stein as a character, the solonière, the nurturer of modernism and friend to Hemingway and Picasso, even the one who coined the term "the Lost Generation," but there was little room for Stein, the most influential American writer of her time.

It should also be noted that Stein and Toklas were expatriates by necessity, only crossing back over the Atlantic once, as older women, with Toklas acting as Stein's "secretary." They couldn't have lived openly as a couple in the U.S., not in Baltimore or Boston or even San Francisco. Their own families would not accept their presence, and neither of them were willing to give up the laissez-faire atmosphere they found in Paris, where they were just peculiar Americans among the French and where they could surround themselves with other men and women like them. By the time they visited in the 1930s, the U.S. was hostile territory for lesbians. A few years later, when they decided to stay and hide out in

6. The New Critics were part of the Southern Agrarian movement that constructed the literary canon for the masses of students who filled the universities in the U.S. on the GI Bill after WWII. Their sense of white superiority was no secret at the time and has recently been foregrounded. See, for example, Miranda B. Hickman and John D. McIntyre's *Rereading the New Criticism* (2012).

Vichy France during the war rather than return to America, they must have carefully weighed the consequences in each nation for two Jewish lesbians who insisted on their right to be together.[7]

THAT IMPENETRABLE NOVEL

"But," some critics and literary historians will protest, "this is not about Gertrude Stein the person. It's about the artist, and that novel. It's just not that good."

"Well," I say, pushing up my sleeves and slicking back my hair. "What do you mean by 'good'?"

This is, indisputably, my favorite topic. As a critic, I constantly poke at the question "How do we know it's good?" In truth, I would not claim to be a Stein expert. Much of her poetry stymies novel-reading me, and there are certainly professors out there who have read more Stein, and for much longer, than I have. But I do know a good novel when I read one. And I will happily (relentlessly) tell you what I mean by that.

Stein's *TMOA* is weird, so weird that John Waters is reading it. In a recent *New York Times* "By the Book" interview, he called *TMOA* "the ultimate bedside book." He goes on: "I enormously respect its impenetrability. Maybe this is the best novel ever written, because you can't read it. Not even two pages. I know, I've tried for the last ten years." I have found, to the contrary, that when you persist, *TMOA* becomes charmingly weird and difficult (like Waters's films). There is a there there. Something is going on, and whatever it is pushes me to read more deeply and examine more carefully.[8] It challenges me to let go of the desire for linear sentences,

7. For further discussion of the accusations of collusion against Stein and Toklas, how they survived Vichy France and the controversy that erupted around it, see Jane Malcolm's *Two Lives: Gertrude and Alice* and Barbara Will's *Unlikely Collaboration: Gertrude Stein, Bernard Faÿ, and the Vichy Dilemma* (2011) and, briefly, our "Biography" section, following this chapter.

8. By far my favorite critical engagement with Stein's novel is E. L. McCallum's *Unmaking the Making of Americans: Toward an Aesthetic Ontology* (2018),

to lose myself in the rhythm of pages and pages of prose that (I know, I know) edge close to nonsensical. Because I read a lot—for a living—I like being surprised. It has become my favorite characteristic of a good novel. Take my breath away, please.

Stein's novel reads like nothing else I have ever encountered, and is, at times, breathtaking in its innovation. Take this passage from an early section entitled "[The Dehnings and the Herslands]," where the narrative conjures its novel readers then speaks directly to them, *Jane Eyre* style, about this book. The novel has just opened with a first-person declaration: "It has always seemed to me a rare privilege, this, of being an American, a real American, one whose tradition it has taken scarcely sixty years to create" (3). It then moves into a more traditional omniscient third person point of view, with an occasional foray back to first person. "That is the story I mean to tell," the narrator inserts at one point, and "We, living now, are always to ourselves young men and women" (3, 4), a phrase repeated, Stein-style, repeatedly—to emphasize her take on "the continuous present" (could there be a more American idea?). Gorgeous circular sentences full of incessant repetition follow, describing the Dehning family, father and mother and children, with a focus on Julia and her "crude domineering American girlhood" at eighteen, with "that crude virginity that makes the American girl safe in her liberty" (15). Then a surprising paragraph-long sentence interrupts the recursive narrative:

> **And so those who read much in story books surely now can tell what to expect of her, and yet, please reader, remember that this is perhaps not the whole of the story either, neither her father for her, nor the living down her mother who is in her, for I am not ready yet to take away the character from our Julia, for truly she may work out as the story books would have her**

particularly the chapter "I Write for Myself and Strangers" where the novel is placed in context of and in conversation with Kant's aesthetic theories. McCallum concludes: "The novel is more about the making than about the Americans. Writing 'for myself and strangers' negotiates 'they' in 'my' perception, which is the basis for that making" (221). The move through Kant's subjective universal to an understanding of the function of repetition (especially of the phrase "As I was saying") is bracing theoretical work.

> or we may find all different kinds of things for her, and so reader, please
> remember, the future is not yet certain for her, and be you well warned
> (16) reader, from the vain-glory of being sudden in your judgment of her.

After this, the text swings back into a third person account, mainly of "our Julia" and her relationship with her father and her fiancée, with never another mention of "vain-glory" in the determinedly simple vocabulary of this section. This passage assumes a familiarity with romance novels, suggesting even a habit of reading "story books" where the marriageable young woman and her choices guide the plot. It conjures a woman reader.

Here's the thing. Since its heralded eighteenth century entry into Western culture, in what we sometimes call "The Age of Reason," the novel has been (and still is) predominantly a woman's genre. As republics were rising, colonialism sputtering, and aristocracies falling, this democratic literary invention rode to success on feminine coattails, with women as its main characters, the majority of its readers, and most of its popular writers. In response to this and other temptations, the tradition of the ladies' conduct book appeared, with fatherly figures—preachers, moralists, essayists—teaching nice young ladies how to behave, in part by discouraging them from novel-reading (while, evidently, encouraging them to read conduct books). "Be you well warned" and "vain-glory" in the *TMOA* passage above reflect their language. Fiction was by nature a lie and, therefore, evil. It let fantasy overtake reason and romance trump duty; it offered readers the chance to experience dangerous adventures vicariously. It gave women ideas.

And yet in spite (or maybe because) of this, by the end of the nineteenth century the little-genre-that-could had staged quite a handy coup. Accessible and engaging, it fit perfectly into populist ideals, and it won audiences over from poetry, essays, plays, the Greek and Latin classics, even the Bible. As I have noted elsewhere, the novel both attracted and constructed the feminine audience that ensured its survival and, finally, its dominance.[9] Today, novels still rule the publishing market, and experts estimate that anywhere between 80–95% of them are bought or read by

9. For further exploration of the gendered history of the novel, see Chapter One of *The Ulysses Delusion*, which I am paraphrasing here.

women. As Ian McEwan wrote in *The Guardian*: "When women stop reading, the novel will be dead."

When Gertrude Stein came of age, then, the publishing market was brimming with successful middle-class women novelists—like Indiana writer Gene Stratton Porter, whose novel *Girl of the Limberlost* Stein chided Sylvia Beach for not carrying at Shakespeare and Company, the famous American bookstore in Paris (Stein also wanted her to stock the classic American western *Trail of the Lonesome Pine*). Even though modernist scholars laugh when we hear this story (of *course* Beach wouldn't have *that* book!), I suspect Stein was only half joking when she insisted it was her favorite. In our strangely undemocratic literary tradition, the division between popular novels and critically acclaimed ones was already growing. And that division expanded further with modernism, when the most praised novels were recognized specifically for being unlike best-selling novels popular with women. In the paradigm-shifting three volume work *No Man's Land: The Place of the Woman Writer in the Twentieth Century*, feminist critics Sandra M. Gilbert and Susan Gubar explore the many ways that modernist writing became the pivot point of a critical war between the sexes, the battle for literary authority, with the novel at ground zero.[10]

Stein was not only aware of the novel's highly gendered history, she seemed eager to work within it as she reconstructed the genre for a new age. Most of her first attempts at writing were novels, and *TMOA* was, again, the work she considered her most important. In *TMOA* she seems to resist the developing critical tendency to dismiss women's novels as less aesthetically and psychologically complex works of art. When she set out to write the first truly modernist novel, rejecting so much of what

10. Sandra Gilbert and Susan Gubar, in *The War of the Words*, the first volume their three-volume feminist study *No Man's Land: The Place of the Woman Writer in the Twentieth Century*, vividly describe "a crisis caused by male dispossession and female self-possession" (34). They write: "In other words, just as more and more women were getting paid for using their brains, more and more men represented them in novels . . . as nothing but bodies . . ." (47). See particularly the last half of the first chapter, "The Battle of the Sexes," for a description of how this played out in novels.

made the traditional realist or naturalist novel work (plot, action, time, setting, even the usual practices of character development), she proceeded respectfully, with attention to the nineteenth-century sentimental novel and its passionate readers, as she indicates through her narrator in the following often-quoted passage:

> Bear it in your mind my reader, but truly I never feel it that there ever can be for me any such creature, no it is this scribbled and dirty and lined paper that is really to be to me always my receiver,—but anyhow reader, bear it in your mind—will there be for me ever any such a creature,—what I have said always before to you, that this that I write down a little each day here on my scraps of paper for you is not just an ordinary kind of novel with a plot and conversations to amuse you, but a record of a decent family progress respectably lived by us and our fathers and our mothers, and our grand-fathers, and grand-mothers, and this is by me carefully a little each day to be written down here; and so my reader arm yourself in every kind of a way to be patient, and to be eager, for you must always have it now before you to hear much more of these many kinds of decent ordinary people, of old, grown, grand-fathers and grand-mothers, of growing old fathers and growing old mothers, of ourselves who are always to be young grown men and women for us, and then there are still to be others and we must wait and see the younger fathers and young mothers bear them for us, these younger fathers and young mothers who always are ourselves inside us, who are to be always young grown men and women to us. [*Note: that was one sentence.*] And so listen while I tell you all about us, and wait while I hasten
> (36) slowly forwards, and love, please, this history of this decent family's progress.

Given the stories we repeat about Stein's masculine presentation and her egotistical assertions of superiority, I particularly appreciate that vulnerable narrative voice she constructs here, so unlike the stereotyped Stein, asking readers to "love, please," this book.[11] The narrator asserts that this is "an ordinary kind of novel with a plot and conversations to amuse you," and

11. Does anyone else hear Julia Roberts?

also "a record of a decent family progress." There is a tacit promise here that in this whirl of words is the kind of novel you're used to, a *Middlemarch* or a *Girl of the Limberlost*, with families simply living their lives. Here Stein is overtly accommodating the novel-reading women that most male-identified modernists will openly reject.[12]

In this passage Stein also charges her metafictional narrator with explaining that this novel will "hasten slowly forward," and so to read it well is "to be patient and to be eager." It doesn't take many more pages for readers to realize that we will need this advice. Stein's elaborations of her writing style claims repetition as her method for developing "ordered recognition" and real familiarity, an unfolding of character and relationships through mundane, daily interchanges. "All men and all women," the narrator explains later, "if they keep on in their living come to the repeating that makes it clear to anyone who listens to them then the real nature of them" (153).

The repetitiveness is interlaced throughout with first-person narrative interruptions. It's as if Stein is offering her readers a backstage pass to the production of a novel. The narrator expresses despair, doubt, curiosity, certainty, disillusionment, loneliness, exhilaration and sadness about the process of writing a book. Paragraph after paragraph begins with "I am thinking"; "I am beginning"; "I'm listening" and, over 900 times, "As I was saying." This open expression of emotion, this bumping up against sentimentality, invites intimacy with the text, as well as with its narrator. The "Martha Hersland" section, for example, begins with the first-person narrator in confessional mode:

> I am writing for myself and strangers. This is the only way that I can do it. Everybody is a real one to me, everybody is like some one else too to me. No one of them that I know can want to know it and so I write for myself and strangers. [...]
>
> There are many that I know and they know it. They are all of them repeating and I hear it. I love it and I tell it, I love it and now I will write it. (317)

12. For further study of how male novelists neglected, rejected, ridiculed and sidelined women readers, see Gilbert and Gubar—and many critics since, including, most recently, novelist Jennifer Weiner's essays collected in *Hungry Heart: Adventures in Life, Love, and Writing* (2017).

Readers participate in character construction by staying with this repetition (patient and eager) until, along with the narrator, we are satisfied that we have begun putting together the puzzle of personality, until we know that the characters are, as the narrator reveals, "quite in me, I am certain" (678). Not that we know them (because we can't) but that we experience them. As the narrator reveals, "Sometime I want to understand every kind of way any one can have the feeling of being distinguished in them and every kind of thing that can give any one a feeling of such distinction in themselves inside them. Sometime I want to understand the complete being in each one" (493-494). This section of the novel is notorious for its taxonomy of human natures and types of being—bottom nature, resisting being, attacking being, "a slow, stupid, gelatinous being" (383). Understanding a person's character, reproducing and not reducing another human being is the greatest storytelling challenge of *TMOA*. And Stein's narrator openly addresses it again and again in these pages.

It's not surprising, then, that this process reveals the narrator as the novel's most interesting character, which might explain why so many critics conflate that voice with Stein's. The prolific Stein could easily be "the writer" who "will go on writing, and not for myself and not for any other one but because it is a thing I certainly can be earnestly doing with sometimes excited feeling and sometimes happy feeling and sometimes longing feeling and sometimes almost indifferent feeling and always with a little dubious feeling" (781). Beginning and beginning again, paying attention to what is revealed in repetition, the narrator demonstrates how reading a book can reiterate the process of writing one. But in the final narrative intrusion the narrator appears to confront the limitations of both text and telling, of understanding and representation:

> I am in desolation and my eyes are large with needing weeping and I have a flush from feverish feeling and I am not knowing what way each one is experiencing in being living [. . .] and I am doing this thing again and again and I am now again and again certain that I will not ever be realising [sic] experiencing in each one of very many men and very many women, I can realise something of experiencing in some of them, in them as kinds of them

> but I am needing to have it in me as a complete thing of each one ever living and I know I will not . . . (803-804)

After this passage, the self-conscious and constructed narrative voice all but disappears, and the text through the "David Hersland" section and the final "History of a Family's Progress" becomes mostly stylized sentences—"typing," as we called it in class. In the U.S., these stylistic practices came to associate the name "Gertrude Stein" with all things modern, particularly after the 1913 Armory Show, the first large American exhibition of modern art. As Professor Susan Hegeman writes, "Stein's emerging reputation was used to promote the show, and the show in turn helped turn the notoriously inaccessible writer into an icon."[13] At the time, this notoriety was a mixed bag of fascination and condemnation, of innovation and incomprehensibility.

To access Stein's writing, however, this link to modernist art can be productive. I keep two postcards of Picasso paintings, both figures of women, inside my copy of *TMOA* as visual reminder that Stein said she was trying to do with writing what Picasso was doing with painting. One, *Portrait d'Olga dans un fauteuil*, 1918, emphasizes that Picasso demonstrated a child prodigy's gift with painting, mastering realism and representation before he was out of his teens; the second, *Portrait de Marie-Therese*, 1937, represents the radical techniques he pursued for the rest of his life—how he deployed his extraordinary skill.

Imagine, then, *Portrait d'Olga dans un fauteuil* as the nineteenth-century women's novel and *Portrait de Marie-Therese* as the modernist novel Stein is inventing in *TMOA*. For me, the centrality of family relationships, the attention to the quotidian, to the feeling of lives dispersed among hindrances, and the aspirational intimacy of this novel's meandering narrative mark a clear path from the nineteenth-century novel to the wildest of modernist experimentation, and from a woman's pen. Just as there are aspects of female figuration through both Picasso paintings, there are recognizable novel conventions throughout *TMOA*. This novel

13. Susan Hegemon writes about the influence of the Armory show on bringing "modernism to the masses" in the U.S.

is not an outright rejection of sentimentality or a forceful assertion of a masculine modernism, stoic and spare. In this way, *TMOA* allows for a more accurate through line in the story we tell about the American novel.

While *TMOA* references the sentimental novel, it is also the jumping off point for most of the artistic twists and turns that became modernism: Stein, by way of her narrator, uses writing as "a form of experience, not simply a way of coming to terms with experience," as Steven Myer explains in his introduction to the 1995 edition (and the 2025 Dalkey Essential edition). The text invites readers to co-construct it, drawing us in with the narrator's attempts to reproduce rather than represent characters; the assertion of a flawed, human, and often unreliable narrator is also a modernist conceit, as is attention to language, to the sounds or words and how to string them together—often in very long sentences. Modernists also experiment with time, as when Woolf, Proust, and Joyce attempt to have their novels move in real time, a day in the life, a page in the hour. In a move paradigmatic of how we came to define modernism, the latter part of *TMOA* sees experimentation completely overwhelm content, and plot and character take a back seat to style. The story becomes "abstract, surreal, collagist," as Stephen Kern describes it in *The Modernist Novel* (165).

Because I have loved novels since I read my first chapter books as a child, I have read a lot of them. I particularly enjoy experimental modernist novels. This is my time period, and these are my favorites. I adore Virginia Woolf's *The Waves*, the poet H.D.'s *HERmione*, and Zora Neale Hurston's *Their Eyes Were Watching God*, with its heady mash-up of anthropology, mythology, and romance. I got lost for a couple of years in Dorothy Richardson's *Pilgrimage*. I admire Hemingway's *The Sun Also Rises*. I had fun with Joyce's *Ulysses* (though I never quite get why critics deem it "the best novel of the twentieth century"). I like reading Faulkner, and have even managed a bit of Proust. And here's the thing: Stein's novel is no more weird or incomprehensible, no less aesthetically pleasing, informed, intelligent, or adept with language than most of the novels we recognize as exemplars of modernism. And even if we write *TMOA* off as a failed novel, it's still an important one, the product of a lively mind engaged in the questions of her day, a thought leader, an influential artist. Her simple, rhythmic language, her challenges to how we experience time and depict personality, her rethinking of the uses of a sentence affected the writers around her and altered the trajectory of American literature.

While conservative cultural forces were certainly at work in denying Stein her central place in American literature, they haven't been *TMOA*'s only roadblock to recognition. The tradition of literary criticism, before and after Stein, has doggedly and consistently sidelined women, refiguring the novel so that its feminine and popular antecedents disappear, then overwriting its history with high-art exemplars; defining modernism as a mainly masculine enterprise, then reimagining Stein's influence as minimal. Without question, aesthetic and literary power struggles affect how we view her work today and which of her texts we pay attention to.[14]

Again, for most of her life, Stein considered *The Making of Americans* her finest work, and she returned to it repeatedly, revising, theorizing, analyzing it. She spent much of her legendary 1934–35 American lecture tour talking about and reading from it. She never wavered in her belief that *TMOA* redefined the novel as significantly as Picasso's work revolutionized visual art, and that it should stand as a pillar of modernism. She was more persistent in seeking a publisher for it than she was with any of her work, serializing it first, at Hemingway's urging, in Ford Maddox Ford's *transatlantic review* in 1924, sixteen years after she completed it, and publishing the impressive tome in 1925 in Robert McAlmon's Contact Collections of Contemporary Writers (see "Publication History"). This novel is, without question, a grand experiment, exhilarating, frustrating,

14. Most of what we know about Stein today is the result of the reclamation work of feminist literary criticism, which appeared in the U.S. simultaneous with the second wave women's movement, beginning in the late 1960s. Many of the scholars engaged in this work have highlighted Stein's influence on the modernist movement, emphatically reaffirming her centrality in its development. But feminist critics also had their preferences; for the most part we leaned away from less accessible texts, those we found less pedagogically useful. Thus, the Stein that students encounter today is often the poet or the author of shorter, more teachable works such as *Three Lives* or *The Autobiography of Alice B. Toklas*. Too often, even for feminist critics, she is the lesbian legend, author of delightful, sexually coded poems, a larger-than-life historical figure rather than a novelist.

influential, constantly challenging and, in the end, brilliant. Winifred Bryher wrote in 1962 that, "It is a measure of the decline of real learning that some people today have questioned [Stein's] genius" (Mellow 291). But question it they have, and *The Making of Americans* has yet to find its place as a central text in our canons of modernism.

HOW TO USE THIS BOOK

I created the Gertrude Stein Seminar because, as an irremediable extrovert, I needed a community to help me work through and understand this long, weighty novel better, to more precisely locate it in the context of the history of the American novel and its mostly women readers. Even as an experienced reader, I couldn't do it alone. Because most Stein scholars work on her poetry or short stories, on the more accessible *Three Lives* or *The Autobiography of Alice B. Toklas*, I was essentially lighting out for the territories, and I needed some fellow travelers to help me sort through what I was reading.

That senior seminar was stimulating and my traveling companions, advanced undergraduates, were strong writers and insightful critics, even though they had little previous experience with modernism. They were always game to tuck in and take on the next 100 pages. They were also, it turned out, ideal colleagues for the trek through Stein's novel. When, with their prompting, we decided to fill the empty space where this book you have in your hands should have been, they were my models of patient, eager readers for *As I Was Saying: A Companion to Gertrude Stein's* The Making of Americans. They became my collaborators. They became the voice of this book, now your own sociable companions through *TMOA*.

My co-author, Janie Sisson, was among those seminar students, as was our collaborator, Emma Hargreaves. Together, we imagined this book into being over two years of work after the seminar ended, rereading, writing, and meeting once a week to check in. Our fondest hope is that this will serve as your seminar, your community support system for reading *TMOA*. And that you will read this novel with at least some of the appreciation we found for it.

In Part One you will find some introductory material—a brief biography of Stein, a history of *TMOA*'s publication and its early reception, and an account of our encounters with early drafts of the novel. We also offer signposts in Part Two, the "Reading the Novel" section—hints for working with Stein's unfamiliar prose style and themes to watch out for, many of them inspired by the Stein seminar.

In Part Three, the heftiest part of the book, we take on as thorough a summary as we could muster from an often plot-free (and chapter-free) book. We hope you will use this to keep reading, reminding yourself what you have to look forward to. We all agreed that this is what helped us most as we made our way through the novel together in seminar. When you inevitably ask (and you will), "What is going on here?" we offer a ready answer, or at least an informed speculation. There is also a list of characters, a family tree (thanks to Emma Hargreaves and Maia LaBrie who sorted out those "strong grandmas" and accounted for "the glutton") and a Bibliography, in case you become as entranced with Stein as we are and want to read more (I particularly recommend the engaging Wagner-Martin biography, which we all enjoyed).

As others have noted before us, *TMOA* has been waiting a long time for its audience and for the serious consideration it deserves. We each know of friends or fellow readers (such as John Waters) who, out of curiosity about the legendary lesbian or in response to others' enthusiasm, committed to reading it, then quickly put it down. We get it. It's a tough text to take on alone.

So let us join you. In creating this book, we aspire to make Stein's great American novel more widely available not just to students and scholars but also to avid novel-readers who are flummoxed by Stein's repetitive and sometimes sleep-inducing style. For you and other adventurous readers we offer *As I Was Saying* as your conversational companion, one seat over, helping to navigate this essential text of American modernism.

Works Cited

* Cody, Morrill and Hugh Ford. *The Women of Montparnasse: The Americans in Paris*. Cranbury, NJ: Cornwall, 1984.
* Boyd, Janet and Sharon J. Kirsch. *Primary Stein: Returning to the Writing of Gertrude Stein*. New York: Lexington Books, 2014. Print.
* DuPlessis, Rachel Blau. "Woofenstein, the Sequel" in *Primary Stein: Returning to the Writing of Gertrude Stein*, Janet Boyd and Sharon J. Kirsch, eds. New York: Lexington Books, 2014. 37-56. Print.
* Evans, David H. "'Never reject anything. Nothing has been proved': William James and Gertrude Stein on time and language" in *Understanding James, Understanding Modernism.*
* New York: Bloomsbury Academic, 2017. (141-160) https://books.google.com/books?id=QNMTDgAAQBAJ&lpg=PA143&ots=8WJDrHmEN3&dq=James%20never%20reject%20anything&pg=PA155#v=onepage&q=James%20never%20reject%20anything&f=false
* Flanner, Janet. *Paris was Yesterday, 1925-1939*. New York: Harcourt, 1972. Print.
* Gilbert, Sandra and Susan Gubar. *No Man's Land: The Place of the Woman Writer in the Twentieth Century*. New Haven: Yale UP, 1987, 1989, 1996. Print.
* Graff, Gerald. *Professing Literature*. Chicago and London: The University of Chicago Press, 1987.
* Hegeman, Susan. "Gertrude Stein and the Armory Show." http://armory.nyhistory.org/gertrude-stein-and-the-armory-show. Accessed 8.15.2017.
* Hickman, Miranda B. and John D. McIntyre. *Rereading the New Criticism*. Columbus OH: OH UP, 2012. PDF (free download).
* Kaufmann, Michael. "Gertrude Stein's *The Making of Americans*: Repetition and the Emergence of Modernism (review)." *American Literature*, vol. 71 no. 4, 1999, pp. 807-808. *Project MUSE*
* Kern, Stephen. *The Modernist Novel: A Critical Introduction*. Cambridge: Cambridge UP, 2011. Print.

* Konchar Farr, Cecilia. *The Ulysses Delusion: Rethinking Standards of Literary Merit*. London: Palgrave Macmillan, 2015. Print.
* Loth, Valérie. *Matisse, Cezanne, Picasso: L'aventure Des Stein*. Exhibition Catalogue (Album de L'Exposition) Paris: Grand Palais, Galeries nationales, 2011.
* McCallum, E.M. *Unmaking the Making of Americans: Toward an Aesthetic Ontology*. Albany NY: SUNY, 2018. Print.
* McEwen, Ian. "Hello, would you like a free book?" in *The Guardian*. 9.20.2005. https://www.theguardian.com/books/2005/sep/20/fiction.features11
* Malcolm, Janet. *Two Lives: Gertrude and Alice*. New Haven CT: Yale UP, 2008. Print.
* Mao, Douglas and Rebecca L. Malkowitz, eds, *Bad Modernisms*. Durham NC: Duke UP, 2006.
* Mellow, James R. *Charmed Circle: Gertrude Stein and Company*. Boston: Houghton Mifflin, 1974. Print.
* Solomon, Jeff. *So Famous and So Gay: The Fabulous Potency of Truman Capote and Gertrude Stein*. Minneapolis MN: U of MN Press, 2017. Print.
* Stein, Gertrude. *The Making of Americans*. London: Dalkey Archive, 1995 (from the 1925 Contact Edition). Print.
* _____ and Sherwood Anderson. *Geography and Plays*. Boston: The Four Seas Company, 1922. Online at googlebooks.com.
* Wagner-Martin, Linda. *Favored Strangers: Gertrude Stein and Her Family*. New Brunswick, NJ: Rutgers University Press, 1995. Print.
* Waters, John. Interview in "By the Book," *New York Times Book Review*. 4.20.2017. Accessed online at nytimes.com.
* Weiner, Jennifer. *Hungry Heart: Adventures in Life, Love, and Writing*. New York: Washington Square P, 2017. Print.

Biography: Becoming Gertrude Stein by Janie Sisson

On February 3, 1874, in Allegheny, Pennsylvania, now the North Side of Pittsburgh, a baby was born to upper-middle class Jewish parents Amelia and Daniel Stein. This new addition to the family easily fit Daniel's ideal of a precious, joyful, and particularly intelligent child, qualities he found lacking in his other four surviving children: Michael, Leo, Bertha, and Simon. So, the newest Stein, Gertrude, referred to as "Baby" by her parents, became the reason for a (fleeting) twinkle in her father's eye.

Pleasing their patriarchal father was not an art the children easily mastered, unless that child was Michael, the oldest of the brothers, and the one expected to eventually take over the family streetcar business. Strong and heavily enforced beliefs about education, success, and money-making clouded Daniel's sensitivities to his wife and children. When Gertrude was just three years old, he whisked the whole family away to Vienna to fulfill his plan for his children to receive a top-notch education (and for his girls to learn to play music). Moving from lavish house to lavish house, the Steins journeyed across Europe in style for a year, accompanied by governesses and tutors.

Their reentry to the U.S. and eventual move to California were not without hindrances. After a stay in Baltimore with Amelia's family (where her first-generation immigrant parents had established a successful clothing store) and a few more quick moves, the Steins finally settled down in a beautiful, spacious home near San Francisco in Oakland—a town that would later become "Gossols" in *The Making of Americans*.

In contrast to frequent tirades from Daniel, Amelia tried to parent the children with gentle understanding, hoping they would notice that she wanted to help them through the demoralizing homelife created by their tyrant father (9).[15] As Linda Wagner-Martin describes her, Amelia was the hero of the family, though rarely acknowledged as such by her children. She mothered them tirelessly, though sometimes ineptly, while managing finances and household expenses and caring for people in the surrounding neighborhoods. Despite being far from her Baltimore family, despite the lack of respect from her children and husband, Amelia consistently took care of others, thrusting her own needs to the side until she could no longer avoid acknowledging her ill health. Diagnosed with cancer in 1884, Amelia slowly deteriorated and died in 1888. James Mellow refers to Gertrude's reaction to her mother's passing as "curiously unfeeling," as Amelia had been ill for long enough that the children had learned to make do without her (25).

Shocking but not altogether surprising to the Stein children, their father passed away from a heart attack three years later, in his bedroom with the door locked. Wagner-Martin describes Leo clambering through the bedroom window to find him. Gertrude, having just graduated high school, had to rely on Michael for financial support. The always reliable Michael sold his father's railroad properties and took responsibility for all of his younger siblings, assisting them with money for basic necessities, college tuition, and, later, an occasional Picasso or Matisse painting.

In 1892, having lost both of her parents in a devastatingly short period, Stein and her older sister spent time at their Aunt Fanny Bachrach's home

15. This first citation comes from *Favored Strangers: Gertrude Stein and her Family* by Linda Wagner-Martin, but our short biography of Stein's life draws on three main sources, for us the most helpful recreations of her life from childhood to the time of her death. Wagner-Martin joins biographer James Mellow, author of *A Charmed Circle*, and Shari Benstock, with excerpts from her *Women of the Left Bank*.

in Baltimore. A strong-willed young woman, Gertrude at first enjoyed living in the confines of her extended family, but quickly realized that learning and education were more important to her than her aunts' standard of marrying and having a family. As Wagner-Martin writes, "Watching [her sister] Bertha taught her that she would rather not lead a woman's life; there was too much disparity between the rewards a woman could expect and those the world gave to men" (23).

Refusing to conform to the mores of the patriarchal society that would force her into heterosexual marriage, she instead followed Leo to Cambridge, Massachusetts, where she continued her education at Radcliffe College.[16] Mellow describes Gertrude's move to Radcliffe after Leo as though she were a "satellite trailing after a superior planet" (27). Yet some biographers and critics discredit Mellow's claim, defending Stein's independence from Leo and insisting that Stein sought, instead, to begin her life as an educated woman.

Among similarly ambitious peers, Stein soared academically in philosophy, literature, and psychology. Her natural inquisitiveness and intellectual ability caught the attention of professors from Harvard University who lectured at Radcliffe College. The philosophy and literature professors who took notice of Stein's capabilities and independent thinking were also among those who, later, most influenced her style. When, in her junior year, she registered for a lecture with William James—later called the father of modern psychology—the two developed a significantly impactful academic relationship. Wagner-Martin asserts that beyond educating her in philosophy and encouraging her to develop emotional connections to art and writing, James also greatly emboldened Stein's self-confidence when he encouraged her to do hands-on experimental work with graduate student Leon Solomons (35).

The work that Stein, Solomons, and James immersed themselves in ultimately led to the widespread interest in what is known today as the "stream of consciousness" style, which the group experimented with under the term "automatic writing," using themselves as the test subjects.

16. Radcliffe College was, at the time, the all-women's branch of Harvard University (then an all men's college).

"Normal Motor Automatism," as it was called, had the team attempting to distract their brains under various conditions, attempting to write without consciously directing the brain in content or context, and seeing what became of it (Mellow 32). Stein's work with James also revealed her drive to experiment with intricate pieces of writing, a drive that, at the time, Stein herself may have not even known she possessed.

George Santayana, a renowned professor of literature and philosophy at Harvard, also had an impact on Gertrude's relationship to words and their meaning. He believed that "words express not simply meaning but attitudes toward meaning" and emphasized that "grammatical structures, not single words, underlie the best expression" (32). Stein worked these methods into her writing, attempting, as Linda Wagner-Martin notes, to search inwardly for the "essence of an experience" and using that "to create language structures that captured the essence" of the feelings associated with that experience (33). The combination of Stein's love for words and their meanings and her exploration with a stream of consciousness style can both be found wound tightly into the structure of *The Making of Americans*.

After passing a Latin exam that had been holding her back from completing her degree, she graduated from Radcliffe in 1898, magna cum laude in philosophy. Stein accepted a place at Johns Hopkins School of Medicine, where she had applied at the urging of James (and some Baltimore family members), despite the fact that she showed little interest in the medical field. At Johns Hopkins, Stein experienced deep sexism and anti-Semitism. Feeling the sharp sting of perceived white male superiority was eye-opening to her; it was so unlike her experience at Radcliffe. Believing in her own academic and intellectual abilities, Stein began exploring human sexuality studies, to further understand the lack of adequate care women received in the medical field. Wagner-Martin introduces Haveock Ellis, a psychologist who wrote the *Studies in the Psychology of Sex*, as the thinker who opened Stein's eyes to the diversity within sexuality and to the idea that such diversity was not morally wrong; sexuality was not inherently fixed within a binary (45). Her research likely cemented in Stein's mind the idea that she was capable of achieving whatever men could. This realization, along with the support and acceptance of her peers, may have been what finally allowed her to see medical school as a waste of her time, at which point she began to fail all of her classes, ultimately dropping out in her last year.

Claribel Cone, a doctor and teacher at Johns Hopkins, youthful, successful, and powerful, became an ideal role model for Stein during this time. Stein admired the way Cone made her aversion to some medical topics known; she was not afraid to argue with male doctors, and she contributed to the medical field exactly as she wanted to, rather than accepting her "place" as a woman—a place male colleagues were eager to remind her of. The presence of strong gender-nonconforming women like Cone in medical school led Stein to become more comfortable exploring her own gender and sexuality. This was messy and confusing to navigate for Stein, and she found herself in what many biographers have called a "love triangle" with classmates Mable Weeks and May Bookstaver, another possible reason for Stein's growing lack of interest in school. As Shari Benstock observes, not only was this relationship constricting, but it also left Stein feeling unable to express her sexuality there in Baltimore as she later would in faraway Paris. "The American experience with lesbian sexuality had led to painful self-doubts and psychological isolation" for her, Benstock writes (14).

With the wind at her sails and medical school in the distance, Gertrude and Leo traveled to Europe in 1902. Gertrude ultimately found London boring and dreary, so she returned to the U.S. without Leo to live in New York with Mabel Weeks and two friends, Harriet Clark and Estelle Rumbold. Here Gertrude penned her first novel, *Quod Erat Demonstrandum*, more commonly referred to as *Q.E.D.*, which featured an American woman as the main character in one of the first coming-out novels in Anglo-American literature.

Q.E.D. is about navigating lesbian romance in a society bent on eradicating and criminalizing it. This realistic novel illustrates how, when a romantic affair between two women develops into a love triangle, loving and longing can become lost in translation because of the restrictions historically imposed on the queer community. The consequences of openly expressing lesbian love were too great for Stein's main character, Adele, to navigate. She can't respond as quickly or openly as the two women she is in love with, and she ends up alone and confused about her own feelings (Mellow 58). Then, like many LGBTQ+ folks, she finds she lacks an outlet to express her true emotions. *Q.E.D.* illustrates the self-shame many LGBTQ+ people experience as a result of internalizing hetero-patriarchy's negative judgments. Stein finished this first novel and sent it out for publication on October 24, 1903. It was no great secret among Stein's friends and readers that *Q.E.D.* was Stein's fictional representation of her relationship with May and Mabel. It is also no great surprise that it went largely unread until 1950, when it was published posthumously.

New York had been important to Stein, serving as the landmark location for her last American sojourn as a young woman. She would only return to the U.S. many years later, as a prominent literary figure. Modernist scholar and feminist theorist Shari Benstock writes, "Even before she left America for the last time, Stein knew herself to be seeking a purposeful life; and she knew that writing was somehow a part of that purpose" (13). So, when Gertrude elected to join Leo in Paris in 1903, she at first had plans to return to America for annual visits. But she never did. The two orphaned siblings make a home together in Paris at 27 rue de Fleurus on the Left Bank, an address that was destined to become one of the best known in the history of American literature.

An unexpected yet memorable moment in the life of the Steins occurred when Michael, having been successful in his business endeavors, let Leo and Gertrude know that that they had enough money in their accounts to last them quite some time. Leo, working to acquaint himself with modern art, had regularly been visiting a favorite gallery, Ambroise Vollard's on the rue Lafitte. Naturally, Leo and Gertrude, the two art aficionados, felt the money burning holes in their pockets and immediately purchased some art—Cézannes, Renoirs, and soon Mattisses and Picassos. Some of these artists were among the many who would later become regular visitors at the Stein siblings' salon on rue de Fleurus.

Gertrude's first impression of Picasso's work was of the painting the *Jeune Fille aux Feurs*, a canvas that Leo preferred and Gertrude found "rather appalling," as she would go on to state in her most well-known book, *The Autobiography of Alice B. Toklas*. Even though the first Picasso paintings she laid eyes on did not impress her, Picasso in person did (with his "rude" banter at a dinner party, which she found rather interesting), and just like that Stein had made a friend for the next forty-one years (Mellow 88). Stein became a distinguished patron of Picasso's artwork, much more so than Leo, and encouraged her friends to purchase and support Picasso's work as well. Picasso's *Portrait of Gertrude Stein*, now an iconic holding in the Metropolitan Museum of Art's collection in New York, originally met with mixed reviews, but Gertrude herself found the painting a perfect representation of her.

Around the time the Steins began collecting artwork, Gertrude started dedicating herself to writing. Early in her time in Paris, she wrote *Fernhurst*, a short fictional depiction of various events surrounding Mabel Haynes's intellectual yet gossipy circle—particularly involving a sticky love triangle between the dean of a college, her protégée, and an unsuspecting male Harvard graduate. This experiment would later be integrated into *TMOA* as part of Martha Hersland's story; Stein had already been jotting notes down for her "long book" (See our chapter on "The Continuous Making of *TMOA*").

In spring 1905, keeping with the theme of modernist experimentation, Stein wrote *Three Lives*, a remarkable analysis of three very different women, one that explores race and sexuality in ways unusual for the time period. By Mellow's account, she also began then to write her "history of a decent family's progress," *TMOA*, a project he refers to as "a queer psychological experiment" in which the author wrote with "more ambition than insight" (114). Gertrude, in time, was to regard the book as her masterpiece, and even more than that, as a benchmark in the history of modernist literature. That a lesbian, gender-nonconforming woman in the early twentieth century remained unerringly proud of her work, work which was ridiculed at every turn, was a feat all on its own.

Stein published *Three Lives* and many short biographic and poetic pieces after that, but she was turned down repeatedly for publication of

TMOA, even by companies that she had personal ties to. Finally, in 1925, after briefly being serialized, Stein's big book was published in full by Contact Press in Paris. The reception was decidedly mixed (see our study of its reception in this section). As Stein scholars Rice and Ulla Dydo write, many (male-identified) critics "turned the tables on her, blaming her for writing incomprehensibly rather than themselves for failing to comprehend . . . anyone reading Stein must understand what it was like for an artist to live under incessant, condescending assaults upon herself as a writer, a person, and a woman" (13). Claiming to know the novel's intentions, a mistake many critics of Stein have made (the author is dead, people!) was reason enough for folks not to read it. (Note: I imagine the male critics reading it while banging a frustrated fist on the table because if a novel is not readable by *them*, it must be some woman's idea of a hoax.) We sometimes wish we could say to Stein, "We're here, we understand," because a century later, the work that needs to be done on behalf of women writers is still not complete. (Imagine her at the center of a modernist GamerGate, surrounded by internet trolls.)

Throughout the years it took for *TMOA*'s eventual publication, Stein enjoyed the unerring support of her life partner, Alice B. Toklas, whom she met in 1907. Much has been made of Stein's romantic relationship with Toklas. Benstock asserts that Stein perceived herself as the masculine force of the pair, a quality easily supported by her dominant personality, as she seemed immediately to take charge of the relationship (16). Further, Benstock and Mellow both maintain that Stein spent her time "gathering the men around her while consigning the 'wives' to other rooms," where they entertained themselves or were entertained by Toklas. These storied behaviors led critics to believe that Stein accepted or even embraced the damaging patriarchal belief that women do not belong in intellectual conversations and should be forced into being domestic supporters instead, because they have no place with the "big boys" at the table.[17]

17. This interpretation, taken from *Women in the Left Bank* by Sherri Benstock (13), assumes that Stein understood herself to be what was then called an "invert," a now outdated term, meaning a fully masculine woman who should have been born a man.

Wagner-Martin's feminist biography paints a more believable picture of the Stein-Toklas partnership: "Neither demanded power from the other; each led in some part of the marriage" (122). Wagner-Martin describes how the two women purposefully *concealed* their romance depending on which guests were visiting, due to the varying degrees to which their friends and acquaintances defied or supported heterosexuality. Discussing Alice's sort of "reconnaissance" of the guests, Wagner-Martin writes, "From the responses, she learned whether visitors could be trusted and, more importantly, whether she and Gertrude could entertain as a couple or would need to separate, with Gertrude staying with the male artists and writers and Alice talking with the 'wives'" (154).

So engrossed were the two in their home and work that they were almost completely surprised by the outbreak of World War I in 1914. Visiting England in an attempt to interest a publisher in *Three Lives* (Stein funded 500 copies herself in 1909), they found their French assets frozen. They hid out in Spain, unable to return to their home in Paris. When they finally returned to the rue de Fleurus on June 20, 1916, the homecoming was bittersweet, as the neighborhood they left was now in dire need of aid—hungry soldiers needed food, citizens gravely sought safety. So, the couple volunteered to assist with the war effort. Stein drove supply trucks to soldiers and civilians, though she sometimes lost her patience with having to push her dead truck, as engine trouble was a frequent occurrence.

Stein and Toklas spent the post-war 1920s famously hosting salons and dinners in their high-walled apartment, "scandalously" filled with modern art. Although Stein's writing still failed to reap financial benefit for them, their parties drew Picasso, Hemingway, Pound, Matisse, and many other famous visitors—and those who wanted to meet them. Stein appreciated these friendships and connections, so she devoted her best efforts to them, favoring relationships over the prospect of getting rich (Wagner-Martin develops this explanation in a passage next to a black and white photograph of a smiling Gertrude staring lovingly at Alice) (149).

In an introduction to Stein's *Geography and Plays*, writer Sherwood Anderson tells of the audacious rumors flying around about his friend Gertrude's personal character. "I had myself heard stories of a long dark room with a languid woman lying on a couch, smoking cigarettes, sipping absinthes perhaps and looking out upon the world with tired, disdainful eyes" (15). This is not, however, what he found. Literary folks and friends recall her laughter filling up a room, her looming form a pillar of comfort rather than provocation. Her artist friends appreciated not only her work and friendship but also her mind.

In spite of her love for them, Stein's friends and visitors had let slip anti-Semitic remarks in front of her for years. While Stein often had the illusion, as the world moved closer to the Holocaust, that anti-Semitism was growing less prevalent, sadness plagued her when she observed the homophobia and anti-Semitism expressed by her American and European visitors at rue de Fleurus (Wagner-Martin 186). Yet, Stein never hid from or expressed shame about her Jewish heritage. And she never denied her love for Toklas. Even so, Stein and Toklas found themselves more frequently leaving their Paris home for the French countryside. Stein soon had her sights set on a manor house in Belignin, near Belley at the foot of the Alps, where the couple moved in 1929, quickly transforming it into their new home. Neighbors could look out their windows and see Gertrude walking her dog Basket or Alice pruning her roses.

There on the sunlit terrace, Stein wrote the first novel that would make her a living, *The Autobiography of Alice B. Toklas*. Benstock points out the irony in Stein's achievement: "Gertrude, obsessed with the question of her own identity, became famous for writing in someone else's voice" (63). Now a published poet and author (and even the writer of a few plays and an opera, *Four Saints and Three Acts*), Stein began to build a reputation in both France and the U.S. She was encouraged by friends and patrons to return to the United States for a lecture tour, and agreed to do so in 1934 (at the behest of her and Alice's empty pockets). There, Stein claimed to have fallen back in love with her country. Lecture tour complete and fanbase growing, Stein returned to Paris, where she wrote of her longing for America and finished her novel, *Ida*, just in time for signs of WWII to grow undeniable. The city became wrought with rumors of war, as Stein and Toklas hastily attempted to remove all of the paintings (104 of them Picassos) from their home. They did their best to keep food on their shelves and supplies at the ready, always welcoming hungry folks into their home. Stein bravely struck deals with black market merchants to find food (often using artwork for currency), and scarcity forced Alice to become a very creative cook. By June 1940, Paris, overrun by German forces, had become completely unsafe for Jews.

The consequences of existing as a Jew in Paris were finally becoming clear to Stein, in spite of her desperate attempts to ignore them. Her Paris living came with utter disconnect. Far removed from the heart of Hitler's war on Jews, Stein and Toklas apparently did not fully understand the dire situation in Germany, but this quickly changed by the summer of 1942 when 50,000 Jews were deported to Auschwitz. Stein's expressed hatred for the Nazis and love of American soldiers appeared in her writing throughout the years of war and after, though she had earlier been openly sympathetic to Marshal Phillippe Pétain, the French leader who tried to make peace with Germany and later collaborated with the Nazis as the head of the Vichy government. After the war, Pétain was tried and convicted of treason, and Stein wrote a letter in his defense. It's also true that Bernard Faÿ, a Vichy official and a dear friend of Stein and other Paris bohemians, protected her paintings from repossession, and, some say, kept Stein safe during the occupation. Faÿ, too, was convicted of collaboration and sentenced to life in prison, but escaped to Switzerland (partially funded by Toklas) and was later pardoned. From these associations, some scholars make a case for Stein and Toklas being collaborators of the Vichy government; others speculate that the two were most concerned with their own safety and desire to stay together; and still others find evidence that they were active in efforts to save Jewish artists.[18] Wagner-Martin writes of this possible collaboration, followed by a passage where she quotes Stein exclaiming that "life is full of contradictions" (247).

When the couple retreated to Belignin, they found that their landlord wanted the house for his son, so they moved to rue de Christine in

18. For a more extensive account of Gertrude and Alice during WWII, see Janet Malcolm's *Gertrude and Alice* and Barbara Will's *Unlikely Collaboration: Gertrude Stein, Bernard Faÿ, and the Vichy Dilemma.*

nearby Culoz, not Switzerland, where they had adamantly been told to go or risk being thrown into a concentration a camp.[19] Soldiers filled the streets even in small French villages, scouring them for Jews, throwing tens of thousands into concentration camps. Starvation was everywhere around them, so Alice shared the yield of her expert gardening. German soldiers required room and board in Stein and Toklas' Culoz home three times, where the two passed quietly as French women. Stein's detailed memories of the war, and her particular affection for American soldiers, can be found in *Wars I Have Seen*, a personal account of her experience.

At seventy-one years old, Stein pressed on, viewing her duty as a public speaker as imperative to her place in the world, so she often spoke directly to groups of soldiers. Yet as the Allies started to pull out of France, Stein's health worsened. She died on July 27, 1946, after surgery for stomach cancer, which she had failed to treat, perhaps not wanting to experience the slow excruciating death her mother endured. Stein's famous last words were to stay with Alice until her own death twenty years later. "What is the answer?" Gertrude asked Alice, who could respond with nothing but silence. "In that case, what is the question?" Stein asks the love of her life, the woman who had stood by her side, surviving patriarchy, sexism, anti-Semitism and repeated loss. She fell into a coma a few hours later. Love is no guarantee of safety, especially as a marginalized, Jewish lesbian in the mid-twentieth century. All of Stein's assets were seized by her family in the wake of her death, leaving Toklas destitute. Toklas relied on her friends for support until her death in 1967.

Without a doubt, Stein's unapologetic insistence on living authentically paved paths for women writers and queer folks who came after her. Ultimately, her willingness to saturate her work with lesbian subtexts, joyful sexuality, and blasts against heteronormative patriarchal society make Stein worth scholars' attention. She shows us that words have power in many forms, and words, much like Stein herself, are not always as they appear. Beyond the attacks on her reputation, the belittling put-downs,

19. Cecilia found on a recent trip that people in Culoz and Belley still point with pride at markers of Stein's presence and are quick to talk about how their neighbors protected the two Americans during the war.

the easy dismissals, and the failures to take her work and her life seriously, Gertrude Stein today remains even more powerful than readers have imagined, and there is so much about her left to explore.

Works Cited

* Benstock, Sheri. *Women of the Left Bank.* University of Texas Press, 1987.
* Martin, Linda Wagner. *Favored Strangers: Gertrude Stein and Her Family.* Rutgers University Press, 1997.
* Mellow, James. *Charmed Circle: Gertrude Stein and Company.* Macmillan, 2003.

Publication History of *The Making of Americans* by Gertrude Stein

1903 Stein begins her Big Book in February, 1903, writing notes and jotting down character ideas in pencil inside tiny, square notebooks.

1906–1908 The original holograph draft followed by the final holograph draft are scrawled in pencil across loose leaf pages and slightly larger notebooks. A notebook containing *Fernhurst* is integrated into the manuscript.

1908–1911 A typescript takes shape with Toklas as the typist and translator of Stein's longhand cursive. Notes from both Stein and Toklas appear on the typescript, along with many edits.

1914–1915 We speculate that it was around this time that Stein made final changes to her typescript, adding and redacting entire sections, pages, and paragraphs. These changes feature an intriguing shift from traditionally popular Jewish and German names into names that were less obviously culturally located, such as the change of the surname Heisman to Hissen and the first name Herman to Henry. Labels of ethnic origin such as "Jewish" and "German-American" are changed to "middle-class."

1924 Excerpts of *The Making of Americans* are published for payment of 30 francs per page in *The Transatlantic Review* by Ford Madox Ford at the request of Ernest Hemingway. The excerpts appeared in nine out of twelve total issues of the literary magazine.

1925 Robert McAlmon's Contact Editions Press & Three Mountains Press agree to co-publish 500 copies of the manuscript. 400 copies are distributed in France, and 100 in the United States.

1934 Harcourt Brace creates the abridged version of *The Making of Americans*, where much of the repetition is removed for the sake of an "easier" reading experience. This edition enjoys wider circulation in the U.S.

1966 Something Else Press publishes the full novel based on the Contact Edition version.

1995 Dalkey Archive Press re-publishes *TMOA* with a foreword by William H. Gass and introduction by Steven Meyer.

Works Cited

* American Literature Collection, Beinecke Rare Book and Manuscript Library, Yale University. "Gertrude Stein and Alice B. Toklas Papers." (n.d.).
* Benstock, Sheri. *Women of the Left Bank.* University of Texas Press, 1987.
* Rainey, Lawrence S. "The Making of Americans (Review)." *Modernism/Modernity* (1997): 222-224.

Early Reception of *TMOA*: "Damned naughty Gertrude" by Cecilia Konchar Farr

ONE THING WE want to emphasize for everyone reading this is that Gertrude Stein dominated American literary modernism in the early twentieth century. There was no one more committed to discovering what the modernist aesthetic, the desire for new forms and approaches, could do to literary writing. Could a novel look like abstract painting or sound like atonal music? Could literature make space for human psychological complexity and a post-Darwinian understanding of our place in the natural world? Could it move as quickly as industrial mechanization or at the newly calculated speed of light?

Yes, she said. Yes, to all of the above. With *TMOA*, Stein set out early in her career to apply an avant-garde aesthetic to her writing, and we believe (as she did) that she succeeded. As we point out in the biography section, she became (in)famous in the U.S. after she published two essays, on Picasso and Matisse, just before the first Armory Show in 1913, in which she introduced modernist painting in modernist prose to Americans (*Camera Work*, August 1912). After that, young writers, as well as painters and other artists, made their way to 27 rue de Fleurus in Paris as they streamed across the Atlantic to participate in this creative movement themselves.

This level of fame and influence is described repeatedly in letters, news stories and memoirs of the day. On the broadside for the Contact

Edition of *TMOA*, Carl van Vechten, a powerful modernist patron and practitioner, calls her "not only the founder of the modern movement in English; she is also at the present time far ahead of her boldest followers." The poet Edith Sitwell, on the same sheet, places Stein "among the most important writers of her time," whose "words are like singing birds flying down upon a branch for a moment." Leafing through a file of reviews of *TMOA* that Alice Toklas, Stein, and others clipped and saved at the time of its publication tells a revealing story about the novel's reception over its first ten years in print. It also offers clues to its subsequent critical neglect.[20]

Let's begin with the reviews that followed the novel's initial (limited but influential) publication in 1925. In Katherine Anne Porter's assessment, "Everybody is Real One" in the *New York Herald Tribune* (1.16.27), she first wants readers to know that she won't be writing about Gertrude the legend—though she is a legend: "Next to James Joyce she is the great influence on the younger generation, who see in her the combination of tribal wise woman and arch-priestess of esthetic." No, Porter insists, she is going to write about the book. She points out first that it was written twenty years ago: "It precedes the war and cubism; it precedes *Ulysses* and *Remembrance of Things Past*." Then Porter locates it as pathbreaking, as a "a very necessary book" and "deeply American." She notes that "without 'movies' or automobiles or prohibition or any of the mechanical properties for making local color, it is a very up-to-date book." But it's Stein's modernist writing style that captures Porter's attention most in this review:

> In beginning of this book, you walk into what seems to be a great spiral, a slow, ever-widening, unmeasured spiral unrolling itself horizontally. The people in this world appear to be motionless at every stage of their progress, each one is simultaneously being born, arriving at all ages and dying. You perceive that it is a world without mobility, everything takes

20. This folder is among the treasures trove of materials in the Gertrude Stein and Alice B. Toklas Collections at Beinecke Rare Book and Manuscript Library at Yale University, the perusal of which heavily informed Janie's and my writing. See: Gertrude Stein and Alice B. Toklas Papers. American Literature Collection, Beinecke Rare Book and Manuscript Library, Yale University.

> place, has taken place, will take place; therefore, nothing takes place, all at once. Yet the illusion of movement persists, the spiral unrolls, you follow; a closed spinning circle is even more hopeless than a universe that will not move. Then you discover it is not a circle, not machine-like repetition, the spiral does open and widen, it is repetition only in the sense that one wave follows upon another. The emotion progresses with the effort of a giant parturition. Gertrude Stein describes her function in terms of digestion, of childbirth: all these people, these fragments of digested knowledge, are in her, they must come out.

Porter also comments on the "intensity of preoccupation" of Stein's writing, "this nearness, this immediacy" that she constructs. "All time is in the present, these people are 'being living,' she makes you no gift of comfortable ripened events past and gone." As characters are developed in "bits and pieces . . . [they] repeat and repeat themselves to you endlessly as living persons do, and always you feel you know them, and always they present a new bit of themselves."

In short, writes Porter, Stein's "efforts to get at the roots of existing life, to create fresh life from them, give her words a dark liquid flowingness, like the murmur of blood. She does not strain words or invent them." While Porter criticizes Stein's "disconcerting break into narrative" in the middle (the "Martha Hersland" section), finding it "full of phrases that might have come out of any careless sentimental novel" and in sharp contrast to "the natural style" of the rest of the novel, she concludes that Stein the writer "is honest in her uncertainties. There are only a few bits of absolute knowledge in the world, people can learn only one or two fundamental facts about each other, the rest is decoration and prejudice. She is very free of decoration and prejudice."

Similarly, the poet Marianne Moore, in a lengthy review published in *The Dial* (80: February 1926, 153–56) calls *TMOA* an "epic of ourselves." She finds it "Romantic, curious, engrossing . . . this story of 'the old people in a new world, the new people made out of the old.'" Moore concludes that "As Bunyan's Christian is English yet universal, this sober, tender-hearted, very searching history of a family's progress, comprehends in its picture of life which is distinctively American, a psychology which is universal."

But these careful and respectful assessments by fellow women writers are the exception among the reviews of *TMOA* in the file. Reading the others, one by one, we were overwhelmed by their overt sexism and by the repeated metaphorical swipes at Stein's size. Take, for example, Willis Steell's review, "An American Novel that Paris is Talking About" in the *Literary Digest International Book Review* (February 1926: 172–3). He begins: "Gertrude Stein has recently published in Paris a book with the title *The Making of Americans*, a book seven and one-half inches wide, nine and one half inches long, and four and one half inches thick. It is printed in small pica type on one thousand pages with narrow margins. Some book!" Leaving the book apparently unopened, the better to measure it, he goes on, "Nothing is easier than to make fun of Gertrude Stein. Ridicule or something worse has been her bitter portion for thirty years." Nevertheless, he laments, she persists. "Her method remains what it was when she first set down disconnected words of one syllable, eliding all 'ifs' and 'ands,' and offering the result as poetry; like a gaunt boulder she stands on her firm base, indifferent whether few or many pass within its shadow."

Unlike Porter, Steell compares Stein *un*favorably to Proust: "Both Marcel and Gertrude find their material in personal recollection, but while the Frenchman is delicately subjective . . . no bull in a china shop could be so destructive as Gertrude is of artistic ideals in her clumsy, objective way." He notes her "desultory wanderings over the face of America," her "mode of progress, one step forward and half a dozen backward," then dismisses her: "Gertrude Stein remains to many literary persons what the hippopotamus was to the farmer, 'no such animal.'"

Paul Rosenfeld in the *Saturday Review* ("Newcomers I. Gertrude Stein," January 2, 1926) also begins with Stein the legend, using this analogy: "The writings of Gertrude Stein stand a massive doorpost in the entrance to the latest American literature." He credits her influence on contemporary writers, how "her use of words . . . made them dare," and even notes that "Joyce of Dublin and the young dadas in Paris" owe their sense of language, "the primacy of rhythm," to Stein. After overviewing (and largely discrediting) her other work, Rosenfeld then takes on *TMOA* and its incomprehensible focus on insignificant women characters:

> [Its rhythm] is heard though static half piffling and half tragic lives, through women whose existences are a series of brilliant beginnings and sudden evaporations; women who lose a lifetime in freeing themselves from family fixations; old maid sisters housing drearily together and circling slowly about their relation to each other; servant girls going through life without heads, serving, wasting themselves, perishing.

Why, he wonders, would *anyone* care about these women?

Perhaps most revealing, however, is prominent critic Edmund Wilson's often-quoted review of the novel (*The New Republic*, April, 13, 1927), where he writes: "I have not read *The Making of Americans* through, and I do not know whether it is possible to do so." He compares it unsatisfactorily to *Three Lives*, which "deserves to be widely read," then accuses Stein of creating "exasperating" and "unintelligible" writing, "queer and almost intolerably boring," concluding that "she has somewhere gone off track": "It may be that she has fallen victim to a sort of metaphysical turn, which, if she had been a man, would have found its play in the elaboration of theory rather than the spinning of abstract fiction." His final assessment calls up not a bull or a hippopotamus but a whale:

> Somewhere the writer of remarkable gifts who created the tragic heroines of *Three Lives* has been sunk in these soporific rigmaroles, in the echolaliac incantations, in these half-witted-sounding catalogues of numbers; but whether the bubbles she sends up from the depths spell out a code we have not yet learned to decipher or whether the washings of the sedentary mind have quite eroded her away, it is impossible for us to know.

By the time the novel is abridged and reprinted by Harcourt Brace in 1934, nearly all traces of respect have disappeared from the reviews, and only the sexist disdain remains. Reviewers dig up Stein's undergraduate papers and accuse her of being in the thrall of psychologist William James and of conducting experiments in "automatic writing" in her fiction—of just letting the pen go and writing without conscious intent. Writer

Conrad Aiken, in *The New Republic* (April 4, 1934) follows that line of argument, calling *TMOA* a "purely 'automatic' book," and suggesting that Stein herself has been duped by James, who had been her professor and mentor years before. The novel is "a fantastic sort of disaster," and "a complete esthetic miscalculation" with rhythm that would be better found "in a tom-tom." An anonymous reviewer in the *Detroit Free Press* (February 18, 1934) calls *TMOA* nonsense and "the subconscious peckings at a typewriter of a lady badly in need of a good rest." Isaac Goldberg, in *Panorama* (Boston, April 1934), raises the stakes, calling Stein "a genius of nonsense," and imagining readers of *TMOA* closing the book and saying, "Good Lord! Is this the gal I slept with last night? I must-a been drunk!"

Ainslie Heewett, writing in the *Louisville Courier Journal* (February 18, 1934), sends up Stein's style in a review replete with both sexist and racist references. Stein, she writes, "cannot paint. Nor draw a line. Knows no art but cooking and needle-work. Can't sing. Or play. Does not care for music. Has no ear." But she "loves words. Words are like potatoes. One can do so many things with words." Stein, she concludes, is just an acolyte, even a construction of William and Henry James. "And their being here is Gertrude Stein." A reviewer in *Catholic World* (April 1934) also attempts to mimic Stein (sounding, ironically, more like Joyce) in one long, unpunctuated sentence ending with "Gertrude stop stop stop mercy mercy stop help help help no use no stop heaven help us poor public Gertrude think try to think try to think poor public public be damned naughty Gertrude mama slap goo goo tootsy wootsy toodel-oo."

These 1934 reviews are, perhaps, best characterized by editor William Soskin's review in the *New York Evening Post* (undated). He praises Stein's influence on Hemingway, then writes not about her work but about her as a person: "I knew a woman once who talked the way this book is written. She was a beautiful woman with a certain physical arrogance about her. She wore Victorian lace when all the magazine stylists were prescribing Schiaparelli clothes—and made you like it. You listened to her." He imagines "a lovely, soft, warm mist about her" as she goes on "to discuss her own husband" over too many highballs, as he nods "understandingly, looking into her eyes." Then: "Gertrude Stein must be something like that woman."

Except she isn't. Not at all—no mist, no husband, no Victorian lace. So, he proceeds to disparage her: "But when Gertrude Stein lumbers on in what her publishers call the power to lay bare the innermost core of souls and things, I give up. I cannot read the stuff. Usually I am a pushover for experimental writing and rather oblique techniques but Stein stops me. Is she a genius? Is she an important influence? I don't know. She's a bore."

The failure of these reviewers to take Stein's experimentations as seriously as those of Proust and Joyce may not have been all due to sexism, but, as these reviews underline, sexism was clearly at work here. Rather than challenge themselves to negotiate the unfamiliar, giving the benefit of the doubt to a recognized aesthetic innovator, these critics toss the book aside and dismiss Stein as inaccessible (and objectionably physically large). Even when recognizing her influence on other writers and artists of the day, even when acknowledging her revolutionary use of language, many reviewers could not accept Stein's pre-eminence in American modernism; so, instead, they worked to undermine it.

The Continuous Making of *The Making of Americans*

On a piercingly cold, grey, and windy day in New Haven, Connecticut, we walked from our hotel to the Beinecke Rare Book and Manuscript Library at Yale University, hoping to view Gertrude Stein's handwritten manuscripts of *The Making of Americans*. Determination and curiosity had gotten us through *TMOA* in our senior seminar nearly three years before, and we carried the same determination and curiosity with us—albeit intensified after having spent many months in between rereading and analyzing Stein's novel. We hoped to confirm what we hypothesized: that Stein engaged in an elaborate drafting process for this novel, with a determined plan and thoughtful revisions that led to the innovations behind the style that changed the course of literature. We wanted to see that process in action so that we could better make our argument—that as a modernist novelist, her influence has been underrepresented. So, an emotional current ran through us as we slowly worked our way through hundreds of pages of penciled cursive.[21]

21. Each notebook, holograph manuscript, and typescript page was numbered by writer, teacher, and Stein scholar Ulla Dydo, at the Beinecke rare book and manuscript library at Yale University where she studied Stein's drafts for several projects, most notably her book, *Gertrude Stein: The Language that Rises* (2003). I use these location numbers in this essay when sharing direct quotes or things we learned from studying Stein's manuscripts of *The Making of Americans*.

Numerous biographers, academics, and critics accused Stein of simply playing with automatic writing, or writing entirely random words on paper and calling it art, in spite of her persistent protests that she was not using automatic writing as she "never had subconscious reactions" while attempting to experiment with it as a student researcher (Mellow 33). Some folks in the literary scene found her ideas fraudulent simply because they didn't take time to understand them. But we knew better as we squinted our tired eyes for hours to decipher the various drafts of the "continuous making" of *The Making of Americans.*

Tiny, worn scraps of paper are, fittingly, the receiver of Stein's brainstorming and plotting, just as her narrator reports in *TMOA.* Flipping (gently) through small, square-shaped notebooks that Stein bought at a shop in Paris, some deconstructed so she could write on them sideways, and decoding her handwriting to the best of our ability, we began to develop an idea of how Stein planned and wrote *TMOA* while evolving her own writing style. Biographer James Mellow got it right when he wrote "*TMOA* was to serve as the laboratory of her later style . . . and even of her habits as a creative writer" (115). This vision of Stein's "Long Book" as a laboratory for style creation and exploration is powerful and (we find) completely accurate.

Even in her earliest drafting stage of *TMOA*, Gertrude Stein brainstormed, made reminder notes to herself, and jotted down character ideas, only to cross them out entirely with large X's scrawled in pencil. It was apparent that the decisions to cut and reassemble entire pages and paragraphs were intentional artistic choices. The persistent presence of gerunds and the melodically rhythmic sentences were already taking shape in a small notebook titled, "Life of Dehnings and Later Life of Herslands." The repetition was not there yet, but there was a familiar echo of the final version of *TMOA* in the carefully simple word choice and the attention to "inner being" types in fictional characters.

Mellow, like many others, accused her of autobiographical moves, of adjusting the number of Stein children and centering herself as the character Martha (114). Yet we learned from studying her notes that Stein reminded herself persistently of each character's personality during her drafting process. Stein wrote reminder notes to herself inside these miniature notebooks, saying things like, "Sort of combine Mable with Helen Butterfield" (755.13) or "Don't describe David till later give his early life without describing" (756.7). Her characters, at some point, had physical descriptions (Can you believe it?). "Alfred and Martha are fair like their cheery little mother," she wrote. "David dark like his father" (756.33). Characters have ages, so that Stein could, as she was writing, locate her characters within a time period, before removing any "realist" information that was not completely necessary to understanding the "bottom natures" of people.

These notes demonstrate that Stein developed each main character with their individual mixture of "being" in mind, mixtures that we do not believe accurately represent Stein's family enough to call the characters "autobiographical." They are fictional, of course, and like fictional characters they possess a blend of the best and worst parts of the human nature that the author observes around her. Stein's characters deal with loss, experience tragedy, build and destroy relationships with one another; their traits, hopes, dreams, and goals, are reflective of their individual experiences and how their repetitive behavior has shaped their lives.

Stein did what she described as "persistently laying out the contrast of the two families" (757.47) in the last of the tiny notebooks, before getting started on the first draft of her novel. Immediately after opening the first holograph draft, we noticed the flowing repetitive sentences, still laced with specifics relating to the contrasting qualities of the Dehnings and the Herslands—and of the individual characters themselves (which led to us constantly poking each other as we found more information: "Oh my god check out this part"). Young David Hersland, for example, has a rather specific romantic life, each of his pursuits listed with names next to them. Both families are similar in that they are "middle class middle class" German-American immigrant families.[22]

22. It is while writing this first manuscript that Stein also composes *Three Lives*, a collection of stories that overlap with *TMOA* among the ideas she jots in her early notebooks. One character from *Three Lives*, Melanctha, makes an appearance in *TMOA* (492).

We also observed that Stein did not always "edit" in the way we think of editing today. She *rewrote*. If she was not satisfied with a chapter, she did not generally change words around to be rewritten again. She simply started over from the beginning.[23] In the section of the holograph manuscript that deals with Martha Hersland, Stein crossed out entire pages that discuss Martha, replacing them instead with many more pages of repetition having little to do with Martha at all.

The second and final holograph manuscript is written in the neatest cursive we had seen from Stein. It is full of intriguing edits—or, at the very least, socio-politically revealing edits. The words "german" and "anglo-saxon" are completely removed, as are descriptions of a "fever" that spread across the nation about how desirable it was to be an "anglo-saxon" gentleman who could follow the ideals of his individual self rather than the ideals of a collective nation.[24] Also removed is the gender of the narrator, who Stein had referred to as "a woman" in the first holograph manuscript via the quote: "I like it that I am feeling that I could be a very happy woman if every one were certain I was a completely wise one."[25] Stories of these two immigrant families are told interchangeably with passages full of beautifully described landscapes (now gone) and perfect standard English punctuation rather than these revised sometimes winding passages of vague descriptive "being" within each character.

The typescript, copied by Alice via typewriter (which, after days of reading Gertrude's handwriting, we considered quite a feat) was called, at the time, *The History of a Family's Progress*. And it features some of the most dramatic changes. Among these passages are stories of Phillip Redfern and Martha Hersland, appearing much more descriptive than the stories that make it into the final version or even the "Fernhurst" notebook she slipped into the final holograph manuscript. Notes of fierce feminism

23. The phrase, "To begin then" sticks with us with a completely new meaning after viewing the rewriting process Stein engaged in while drafting *TMOA*, realizing that she did, indeed, begin again . . . and again.

24. Final holograph manuscript, chapter 1.

25. Holograph draft, (1590–1600)

surround Martha Hersland as she separates herself from Redfern, and Stein removes passages about the "danger" women possess within them, the danger unleashed on the men who wrong them, in this case, Redfern (who is described as possessing "his intelligent face and tall clean built American body").[26] Here, too, Stein removes the reflections on women's colleges, and lets the Fernhurst manuscript go, renaming the college and most of the characters associated with it.

It is clear from the typescript that Stein was concerned with rhythm, particularly the way the absence of words with short syllables changed the rhythm of the sentence flow. She begins to add words like "very" before words like "many" to create rhythm, so what was once "many others" becomes "very many others" or a sentence modified from "some are in the middle of their middle living" to "some are in the middle of the middle of their middle living," and we can see how this rhythm she is trying to create takes form in both the final version of *TMOA*, and her later writing.[27]

These earlier manuscripts are also much more concerned with the sexuality and gender of their characters. It is no secret by this point that the narrator is non-gendered, but many of the characters' love interests begin with genders and sexualities that are specified in the earlier texts. Stein does not stick to this pattern, and the modernist vagueness that touches the main characters names and life events also reaches their romantic preferences in the final version of *TMOA*.

That cold day in January stays with us still, along with the feeling of anticipation that inspired us in the months after, as we expanded and modified our understanding of the novel through the revelations in its early versions. We constructed, as well, a revised image of Stein through these manuscripts (and from the many photos in the files), a comforting vision of her solid form bent over her desk in Rue de Fleurus in the middle of the night, away from those who would criticize or interrupt her work during the day. Her incessant beginning again, her rewriting, and the persistence of her revision reveal her character. Self-driven and highly

26. Holograph draft (1052–1053)

27. Typescript 1044

motivated, supported by Alice but few others, she edits, deletes, creates and recreates, until the version of *The Making of Americans* you are setting out to read now grows into the literary project that Stein was, thereafter, most proud of—her "beginning, really the beginning of modern writing."

Part Two:
Reading the Novel

Chapter One
The Narrator They:
Metafictional Authorial Intent

Of all the pioneering aspects of Gertrude Stein's modernist writing, her metafictional narrator in *The Making of Americans* may be the most innovative. Patricia Waugh, author of *Metafiction: The Theory and Practice of Self-Conscious Fiction*, refers to the metafictional phenomenon as a development in theory where a novel "self-consciously and systematically draws attention" to its own existence as a piece of artwork. Though narrative intrusions and the narrator-as-character have often appeared in the three hundred-year history of the novel as a genre, metafictional novels allow readers to interact with and reflect on texts in new ways, posing questions "about the relationship between fiction and reality." Stein's elusive narrator in *TMOA* challenged realist literary norms well before metafiction was a term in general use; Stein's narrator occupies an in-between place in the text, acting as a link between the story and the "real world" in ways not common in early twentieth-century literature.

Breaking from established patterns, even metafictional ones, Stein creates a narrator who is not a wise, controlling voice interjecting occasionally to refocus us or to remind us that we are reading a work of fiction, but one who is, instead, an often insecure and flawed human, ardently (sometimes relentlessly) begging us to please listen to this story about an ordinary family's progress. This narrator is also purposefully not gendered; all references to gender, some masculine, some feminine, were removed in the novel's early drafts. We chose, as a result, to follow Stein's direction and reject the gender binary for our narrator; we use they/them pronouns in this book when we refer to the *TMOA* narrator.

The narrator, also self-identified as the novel's "writer," undermines the realist traditions of both first-person and omniscient narrators who reveal what readers need to know to understand the story in front of them. Stein's narrator does the opposite, emphasizing their own feelings repeatedly, going off on long tangents about seemingly insignificant secondary characters (mostly women), and barely telling readers what they need to know to make sense of any possible plot. In some ways, the narrator can make reading this novel even more challenging, particularly the first time through. Through passages like this one, readers quickly learn that we should entirely let go of our narrative expectations:

> Bear it in your mind my reader, but truly I never feel it that there ever can be for me any such a creature, no it is this scribbled and dirty and lined paper that is really to be to me always my receiver,—but anyhow reader, bear it in your mind—will there be for me ever any such a creature,—what I have said always before to you, that this that I write down a little each day here on my scraps of paper for you is not just an ordinary kind of novel with a plot and conversations to amuse you, but a record of a decent family progress
> (36) respectably lived by us and our fathers and our mothers. . . .

Sure, many narrators have their identity concealed, but this narrator has the outward markings of identity stripped away entirely, even while appearing emotionally present and alive to readers. There is no sexuality, no gender, no embodied physical description, only feelings and ideas—only the writing process and their opinions about it; only this "decent family" they describe for us. Stein constructs a narrator who is also the writer, while studiously omitting the image of herself as the person behind the writing. And, correspondingly, the reader becomes conceptual, simple scraps of paper.

Stein's narrator/writer unapologetically inserts themself into the story. And while realist narrators generally act as literary tour guides, supervising the story with a godlike air, Stein's narrator, in stark contrast, experiences internal moments of complete and utter failure. They don't know anything, despite pouring hours of fervent effort into documenting each type of being in all men and women:

> I am all unhappy in this writing. I know very much of the meaning of the being in men and women. I know it and I feel it and I am always learning more of it and now I am telling it and I am nervous and driving and unhappy in it. Sometimes I will be all happy in it. (382)

Lew Welch, author of *How I Read Gertrude Stein*, argues that as Stein's narrator both feels and expresses unhappiness over the artwork they created, they reveal themself as no different from any artist giving up on a canvas or any writer throwing away a crumpled journal page. The only difference is that Stein's narrator is honest with readers about it. They leave the crumpled page in. They let readers see the process, taking us along for the (bumpy) ride of artistic creation.

Another difficult aspect of Stein's choice of a metafictional narrator is that it allows the construction of purposeful authorial intention, something traditionally withheld in all but didactic stories. But teaching is not on this narrator's agenda. Their motivation is, evidently, love:

> There are many that I know and they know it. They are all of them repeating and I hear it. I love it and I tell it. I love it and now I will write it. This is now a history of my love of it. I hear it and I love it and I write it. They repeat it. They live it and I see it and I hear it. (319)

Because their understanding is presented as so obviously in process, the narrator dredges up questions of reliability for the reader. How credible can we assume Stein's narrator is when the question of intent is so present in these metafictional passages? The constant reminder of "as I was saying" seems a repeated reestablishment of authority, as if the narrator asserts credibility through telling us, "I'm here! I don't know everything, but I'm still here." And while it certainly reinforces connection to show and share vulnerability, does it make the narrator more or less credible for readers? We have to decide.

Reading *TMOA*, you can't avoid the narrator—even if you want to. This never-ending presence adds an offbeat assertiveness, a sometimes irritating insistence, to the narrator's voice. How many "as I was sayings" are in here again? The answer is (a completely necessary 955). "As I was saying" reinforces the importance of repetition:

> I am writing for myself and strangers. This is the only way that I can do it. Everybody is a real one to me, everybody is like someone else too to me . . . It is very important to me to always know it, to always see it which one looks like others and to tell it. I write for myself and strangers. I do this for my own sake and for the sake of those who know I know it that they look
> (317) like other ones, that they are separate and yet always repeated.

Repetition draws out character for this narrator, whose encompassing affection touches all of the characters and readers, even strangers, even those with "stupid being" in them.

Yet, the narrator refers to themself as possessing the quality of singularity, a pervasive oddness that cannot be ignored even by a casual observer. Choosing to forgo any gender identification, Stein's narrator instead introduces themself by announcing and identifying their lonely place in society's small pool of people who possess "vital singularity":

> How singularity that is neither crazy, sporty, faddish, or a fashion, or low class with distinction, such a singularity, I say, we have not made enough of yet so that any other one can really know it, it is as yet an unknown product with us. It takes time to make queer people, and to have others who can know it, time and a certainty of place and means. Custom, passion, and a feel for mother earth are needed to breed vital singularity in any man, and
> (22-23) alas, how poor we are in all these three.

It seems that Stein purposefully employs the word "queer" here, which, thanks to the scandal of Oscar Wilde's same-sex relationship with the son of the Marquess of Queensberry, already carried negative heteronormative weight in the early twentieth century. Here we see the narrator refusing again to take on a gender, even as they go on to discuss how their "brother singulars" exist on the edges of polite society. Yet they celebrate these singulars; they do not want to waste time listening to others who are critical of them, or to those who say they are "misplaced in their generation."

In the end, what does this deliberate narrative masking and failure to gender do to your reading of this novel? It certainly makes picturing a person behind the voice a bit more tricky. For us, it made the separation of Gertrude Stein from the narrator easier. But it also made it more difficult to place the narrator inside the story, as one of the characters or even as one of their relatives. If anything, the narrator ends up working at cross-purposes with the story, literally deconstructing the "progress" of this family, as no one (literally no one) succeeds in their patriarchal, heteronormative endeavors. Gavin Craig, author of *Language, Plot and Being Mistaken*, posits that Stein uses the voice of an ambiguous narrator to resist the demands of post-eighteenth-century literature plots, linear as they were, resolving into marriage and heterosexuality—and oppression. Craig also proposes that, eventually, readers really want to hear from the narrator, and we wait for those interjections to keep us going. That was certainly true for us. At some point, before disappearing near the end, the narrator became our favorite character in *TMOA*.

Whatever else can be said for this narrator, their presence draws us into the act of writing. They demonstrate what it takes to make a novel, to keep going even when it seems impossible, to try and create believable characters who are "full up" in contexts of multiple relationships, and to let language sing. Because we know that Stein spent two significant years working fiercely on *TMOA*, writing its 1,000-plus pages out longhand in notebooks and across sheaves of paper two and three times, we know that the background for her writing was alive with talk of developing modernism, of new movements in the visual arts. These years, 1906–1908, were the years when the Stein family made waves in the Paris art scene with their collections of modern art, the years when Gertrude visited Picasso's studio nearly one hundred times to sit for her now-famous portrait.

For this reason, we are convinced that Stein aimed to reject traditional representation and to emphasize artifice the way these painters were doing. She worked to reveal the basic elements of art, to exert the significance of character development, of the passing of time, of the primacy of language as a medium. And she managed this modernist repositioning by creating a narrator unique in the history of American literature, one who lifts the realist veil on the structures and techniques of novel writing the way modernist art reveals the basic elements and concepts of the visual. Full of emotion—of despair and love and sometimes shocking self-confidence—this narrator draws us into the human drama in front of us, truly "being living" as they help us to see it, love it, and read it.

Chapter Two
The Modernist Sentence: *"They are all of them repeating"*

Like many of today's celebrities, Gertrude Stein, in her time, was famous for being famous. Though few people read her work (before the 1933 publication of *The Autobiography of Alice B. Toklas*), many had encountered snippets of her word portraits and poems and had heard she was a character, a bohemian original. For many readers, particularly in the U.S. after WWI, Stein's writing charted the edges of "modern."

Her style appeared as a provocation. Like abstract art, it taunted the conventional. Employing traditional modes of reading, it was near impossible to make sense of. And, as we saw in the critical response to *TMOA*, that made some reviewers mad—recall Edmund Wilson's exasperation at her "unintelligible" writing or William Soskin's declaration, "She's a bore." Repetition and twisted syntax might be tolerable, even charming, in a short poem or magazine article, but not in a story of any length, and certainly not for a novel. Stein-ian style is where even twenty-first-century readers run into roadblocks. So, anticipating the frustration in your encounters with reading *TMOA*, we want to offer a few hints.

If we started by mapping what many, many critics have written about Stein's style, you would never get to the novel itself, so, as your reading companions, we want simply to share what helped us make sense of Stein's prose as we read *TMOA*. So, we begin by invoking Ulla E. Dydo, the undisputed Dean of Stein Studies, who asserts that Stein's entire project was always a "rejection of the rigid conventions of language [that] led her gradually to dissociate herself from all inflexible forms, including hierarchical thinking, authoritarian organization, prescriptive grammar, and chronological narrative—aspects of the patriarchy." Marianne DeKoven, too, identifies Stein's experimental writing as "anti-patriarchal"—and "anarchic, undifferentiated, indeterminate, multiple, open-ended" (xvi, xvii). These critics see Stein's work as a radical project; Dydo concludes that, "In a sense, all her work is a demonstration of possibilities of grammar for democracy. She was interested in spacious, living sentences" (17). This echoes our sense of *TMOA* not as an elitist project but as a disruption, a wholesale reinvention of literary conventions. And we love the idea of "spacious, living sentences."

Those sentences, though. There are a lot of them, and many of them are a lot like other ones. We begin with repetition because that is the barrier that often blocks readers' passage through this novel. Most of us are familiar with Stein's famous quote, "A rose is a rose is a rose." Dydo argues that Stein wanted to "free words," and one way to do this "was to remove them from habitual associations and treat them as things rather than as signs. Repeating a word over and over gradually breaks the bond of word and reference. A form of punning, repetition gives body to the word and assaults meaning" (16). Stein famously insisted that she invited readers to see the rose as *thing* for the first time in "a hundred years" and to make it red. But we suspect she also wanted us to make it read, to invite us to see the word as a *word*, to hear it and register it as a construction of language.

Throughout the novel, then, Stein forms sentences that highlight, de-center and re-center individual words. For example, in several passages at the beginning of the Martha Hersland section the narrator connects their love of observation with their style of writing—both orbiting around the word "repeating": "There are many that I know and they know it. They are all of them repeating and I hear it. I love it and I tell it, I love it and now I will write it" (317). Then, two pages later: "There are many that I know and they know it. They are all of them repeating and I hear it. I love it and I tell it. I love it and now I will write it. This is now a history of my love of it. I hear it and I love it and I write it. They repeat it. They live it and

I see it and I hear it." (319). And again: "There are many that I know and they know it. They are all of them repeating and I hear it. More and more I understand it. I love it and I tell it. I love it and always I will tell it. They live it and I see it and I hear it" (321). The verbs—know, hear, love, write, understand, tell, and, of course, repeat[ing]—leap off the page (see how the typeset appears to get more uniform, how it lines up, how it *looks*?); Stein emphasizes them again and again, persistently, and throughout the novel. Sometimes they fall into lists that are then arranged and rearranged: "There are many ways of thinking feeling knowing believing in many men and women in all there ever are or were or will be of men and women." And a paragraph later: "There are many then believing thinking knowing feeling doing things, mostly every one is feeling knowing thinking doing something, doing feeling believing knowing thinking a very great many things . . ." (546).

These sentences both call us to increased attention—to the small tweaks she makes in each iteration—and also lull us into inattention with their rhythms. They meander unpunctuated and won't allow readers to pin them down with subject-verb-object meaning-making. We shift our attention to order, to sounds, to placements on the page. Somewhere in the challenging David Hersland section, between reiterations of "certainly" and "being living," the reappearance of the habitual "As I was saying," becomes a welcome reorientation, a reconnection to the eccentric narrator. When a string of adjectives ends with a reassertion of those familiar verbs, it produces a similar effect:

> . . . how quickly and how slowly, how completely, how gradually, how intermittently, how noisily, how silently, how happily, how drearily . . . how persistently, how repeatedly, how repeatingly, how drily, how startlingly, how funnily, how certainly, how hesitatingly, anything is coming out of that one . . . makes of each one one meaning something and feeling, telling, thinking being certain and being living. (864)

Again, this novel was Stein's first serious writing project, an ambitious experimentation that grew out of her desire to create a literary style that echoed the ambitions of the visual artists she encountered in Paris, one that answered the call of new century to "make it new," as the modernists later demanded of their movement. It helped us as we read to imagine words as her modernist palette—impressionist, fauvist, cubist words—and to observe how she invites readers to understand them differently as she puts them into sentences that look like nothing anyone had seen before.

Another unique characteristic of Stein's style in *TMOA* is its effort to create a sense of "continuous present." We began our Stein seminar with Stephen Kern's accessible introduction to *The Modernist Novel.* In it, he describes the elevated attention to space and time, the "valorization of the present," that characterized the modernist narrative. "In contrast to the realists' fluid movement of stories from past to present to future, modernists often focus on the present," he writes (101). This shift in perspective, in temporality, was part of a strategy for finding "new ways of seeing and interpreting the world, and narrative forms are the literary manifestation of those ways" (2).

Throughout the novel, the present moment leads its Herslands and Dehnings along from young adulthood, where "we are always to ourselves young men and women," through their aging and, finally, unimaginably, to their deaths. Spiraling around this present like a helix as it "hastens slowly forward" are the future and the past—the good grandmothers, parents, siblings, servants, friends, and lovers. Twisting it together is our narrator, resisting the passage of time even while accounting for it, promising to get to their story (and promising again: "This will now be a history of him . . ."; "Now to slowly begin . . ."; "To begin again . . ."), then turning aside, wandering away and, again, returning. In her *Lectures in America*, Stein attempts to explain this pacing:

> I am always trying to tell this thing that a space of time is a natural thing for an American to always have inside them as something in which they are continuously moving. Think of anything, of cowboys, of movies, of detective stories, of anybody who goes anywhere or stays at home and is an American and you will realize that it is something strictly American to conceive a space that is filled with

> moving and my first real effort to express this thing which is an American thing began in writing *The Making of Americans*. (161)

She also claimed to have been "completely possessed by the necessity that writing should go on," so her use (or nonuse) of punctuation and capitalization had to do with writing going on, "which was at that time the most profound need I had in connection with writing" (217).

Consider, for example, this brief description of the relationship of the Hersland parents, David and Fanny:

> In his earlier living when she first was a wife to him she was a little outside of him she could a little affect him she could a little resist herself to him, she was then in him a beginning as a tender feeling, she was then in him a little like a flower inside him, she was a little then outside him to him, she was then a little important to him as outside him, more and more then this came to be a joke to him, later then she came to be brushed away from around him. (169)

Note how, in the first line, Stein chooses the verb "living," a present participle form that moves the character through time, rather than the more predictable "life," a noun that solidly occupies only that space. The paragraph then takes the couple through the entirety of their time together while also fixing itself in a moment, in their country house in their "middle living."

Progressive verbs abound in this novel and are sometimes doubled in awkward assertions of a present moment—now "being living" or "realizing experiencing." Until the characters encounter death. Then "dead is dead," and a character becomes a noun—"a dead one." David Hersland's life is recounted by way of his "being and listening and talking and being liked and disliked and remembered and forgotten and going on being living and dying and being a dead one" (801). Even when he is gone, we move on in the moment, remembering across time "his having been a dead one, his having been a living one" (999).

Our final recommendation for how to make sense of Stein's sentences was our own, but we discovered, after sharing a conference panel with

Stein scholar Ellen McCallum, that it is a widely shared strategy for reading this novel: When all else fails, read it aloud. There is real oral quality to it, a sense of the sound of words that often had us laughing out loud as we pronounced the sentences. How could anyone resist the repeated reminders that "stupid being is in everyone" or her attempt to give substance to "attacking being," as "a pulpy not dust not dirt but a more mixed up substance, it can be slimy, gelatinous, gluey, white opaquy kind of thing and it can be white and vibrant, and clear and heated and this is all not very clear to me and I will now tell more about it" (383)? Allen Ginsberg once wrote in the *Village Voice* that "The masters of the Berkeley Renaissance read Gertrude Stein aloud and practiced Poetic kabbalah" (December 12, 1968, XIV/9). So, really, why wouldn't we?

But we also want you to know that you can have Stein read Stein aloud to you. Recordings of her reading passages of *TMOA* have been digitized and are now available online, including a rich trove from the archives at the University of Pennsylvania whose provenance dates to a taping at Columbia University during her 1935 U.S. lecture tour (writing.upenn.edu/pennsound/x/Stein). You don't know what you're missing if you haven't heard Stein intone repeatedly about repeating or reminding you pleasantly of your mortality, that "everyone can come to be a dead one." If that's not sufficient, take a minute (or five) to listen to her reading "If I Told Him: A Completed Portrait of Picasso."

Go. Go now. Then come back to *TMOA* with that voice in your ears. That's the best advice we have for negotiating the Steinian sentence.

Chapter Three
On Being American:
Geography, Nationality and Class

One of the most helpful things to remember as you take on this novel is that Gertrude Stein wrote it as a meditation on what it means to be American. Only recently an expatriate, she had spent her formative years in California, Massachusetts, and Maryland, but she had yet to encounter herself as "an American" the way she must have in her early years in Paris, the way many people do when they first travel or live abroad. In fact, the beginning lines of the novel are:

> It has always seemed to me a rare privilege, this, of being an American, a real American, one whose tradition it has taken scarcely sixty years to create. We need only realise our parents, remember our grandparents and know ourselves and our history is complete.
>
> The old people in a new world, the new people made out of the old, that is the story I mean to tell, for that is what really is and what I really know. (3)

We know that Stein began to formulate the ideas for *The Making of Americans* in scattered scrawls through her notebooks as early as 1903, the year she moved to Paris, and that it held the full focus of her artistic attention for two years, 1906–1908. When she got to Paris, like Hemingway and other expatriates who would come later, she wrote first about the U.S.—in the vignettes about women that became *Three Lives*, her first published work. Then she set her sights on *TMOA*. Among all the stated intents of this work, then, writing about America was observably at the top of her agenda.

Imagine her setting off from 27 rue de Fleurus walking past buildings that were hundreds of years older than the nation she came from. With both parents dead, she and her brother Leo were living unmoored from any pressing family ties; her own history, then, became short, as she began to articulate an identity linked to her immigrant grandparents and their act of leaving the Old World behind. There in Paris, at the heart of the Old World, she was decidedly American, young, eccentric, and full of new ideas. Determined to write her truth, she began constructing a history as truncated as hers—three generations. That's all it would take to tell her own story, and it was all it took to tell the story of the American family that would become *TMOA*.

Much of what identified "American" outside of the U.S. in those early days of the nation were landscapes—vast, unpopulated, epic—like the ones in paintings by Thomas Cole and novels by James Fenimore Cooper. Even now, the iconic lands of the American West fascinate international travelers as they make their way to the photo-ready backdrops of its deserts, canyons and red rock formations. In early drafts of *TMOA*, Stein followed that tradition, as she described in uncharacteristically florid detail the "the concentrated starry meadows of New England," the "rich flowering uplands of the rural South" and the "Spanish desert places of the West or the bare sun-burned foot hills of California." But when she revised the novel, honing her style, she cut out nearly all references to setting. Representation of "American-ness" came, instead, through the characters and the "accomplished harmony between a people and their land" (First Holograph Draft).

This harmony is found in the way the Dehning family lives "pleasantly, quite entirely decently, not very aggressively, pretty freely, quite contentedly, fairly advancedly, thoroughly generously, quite gaily, pretty entirely cheerfully, right very rich american living" (686). And it's repeated in the depictions of the Hersland family's life in Gossols and their own version of "rich american living" on a fruitful ten acres where "no other rich people were living" (122). In this pocket of Western geography "they had a little grain and fruit trees and vegetable gardening, they had many kinds of trees and sometimes they chopped down one of them, they had dogs and chickens and sometimes ducks and turkeys in the yard then, they had horses and two cows and . . . sometimes they had rabbits and always they had dogs . . ." (136). At one point, Mr. Hersland decides to give his children a vigorous American education, connecting them to that land rather than Old World culture: "They were american, they did not need french and german, they did not need to bother about music then, they could do that later, now they needed strength and gymnastics and out of door living, and swimming and shooting" (264).

In the novel, Martha Hersland carries the legacy of that American upbringing with her when she goes off to college at "a typical coeducational college of the west, a completely democratic institution" where Martha was among many "vigorous young women" (475). No one there cared "how any man or woman came by the money that was educating them, whether it came through several generations of gentlemen to them, whether it came through two generations or one, whether one of them earned it for herself or himself by working, or teaching, or working on a farm or at a book-selling," thus making democracy "really almost complete among all of them" (475).

Stein herself famously explained her commitment to this democratic vision in *The Autobiography of Alice B. Toklas*: "The important thing is that you must have deep down as the deepest thing in you a sense of equality" (174). Later, the writer Sherwood Anderson would describe this attitude as characteristic of Stein's writing. She lives, he notes, "among the little housekeeping words, the swaggering bullying street-corner words, the honest working, money saving words and all the other forgotten and neglected citizens of the sacred and half-forgotten city" (Introduction to *Geography and Plays*).

But for all of the text's attention to working- and lower-class characters, governesses and seamstresses, and poor people, the emphasis in this "History of a Family's Progress" is on the expansive American middle class through its focus on two immigrant families on the rise. This is emphasized by the voice of a narrator/author who affirms the middle class as central and universal. "I take a simple interest in the ordinary kinds of families, histories, I believe in simple middle class monotonous tradition, in a way in honest enough business methods," they claim early on (37). By repeatedly restating their belief in the "simple middle class tradition" the narrator hunkers down into that space as well, speaking for and from the American middle class.

But this space is not without pitfalls. Women, especially marriageable young women, need to balance carefully the appearance of both monotony and "singularity." Julia Dehning, at 18, is described as showing all the "vigor, the self-satisfied crude domineering American girlhood that was strong inside her," of attaining "that crude virginity that makes the American girl safe in all her liberty" (15). The narrator instructs:

> There can be nothing more attractive than a strain of singularity that yet
> keeps well within the limits of conventional respectability a singularity that
> is, so to speak, well dressed and well set up. This is the nearest approach
> the middle class young woman can ever hope to make to the indifference and
> distinction of the really noble. When singularity goes further and so gets
> to be always stronger, there comes to be in it too much real danger for any
> (22) middle class young woman to follow it farther.

The narrator suggests that in order to attain her highest distinction as an American middle-class female, Julia has to disguise her individuality and uniqueness and dress herself up in conventional respectability so she can achieve what is expected of her—to get married.

The persistent narrator provides another example of middle-class limitation when they explain that Alfred, as the oldest Hersland son, on his way to being Julia's future husband, often feels a responsibility to protect his siblings from both rich children and poor ones. For example, when "children living the rich American living" came to visit the Hersland ten acres, and the "Hersland children had to play and talk with" them, "Alfred had not any liking for them." In fact, Alfred "liked to have all the fruit picked even before it was quite ripe before it was really ready for picking so that those children who were coming to visit them should not be using their trees to pick fruit and enjoy it" (582). Yet, as he gets older and starts to feel the weight of his position in the family, he steers his older sister Martha away from their childhood friends, the poor people "living in small houses" near them in Gossols (580). He knows that Martha's "future living would be a different one from anything that any of them would naturally be having" (581).

Does the narrator judge the narrowness of this middle-class vision, or hold it up as exemplary? Do they own its values or expose them? It's really impossible to say, since they represent different characters' perspectives and come down in different places as we move through the novel. As you read, you may be brought to a screeching halt, as we were, by dismissive or insulting comments about the poor or lower-class people the text describes, like the ones "in the small houses" in Gossols. The narrator sometimes seems astonishingly smug. In a short treatise on "the American teaching" on "loving and marrying" in the first section of the novel, for example, they offer the judgmental observation that such teaching is "very well for young people or for poor ones or for those who are strong in a sense of loving, who have a lively sense of wanting, who have strongly the instinct for mating, but for most of them, the well to do, comfortable men and women, it takes more to make a marriage for them" (74). To follow the "right way of living," marriage can't be simply about loving, wanting, or mating. In fact, in our reading we found the most apparent rejection of middle-class values in the failure of Julia and Alfred's perfect "right American" marriage. Marriage between a man and a woman is a typical middle-class value, one that girls are often taught is a culminating point in their lives, but in this case, the value does not survive the marriage. "The Herslands Alfred and Julia Hersland did not go on being in married living. It was a natural thing as I was saying that they should not be succeeding in married living, the two of them" (740). It's that simple. It just didn't work—never did, never would.

In the end, we were left with a strong impression from this insistent passage, where the narrator we met on the novel's first pages reappears to speak directly to the reader, using "I" statements:

> Middle-class, middle-class, I know no one of my friends who will admit it, one can find no one among you all to belong to it, I know that here we are to be democratic and aristocratic and not have it, for middle class is sordid material unillusioned unaspiring and always monotonous for it is always there and to be always repeated, and yet I am strong, and I am right, and I know it, and I say to you and you are to listen to it, yes here in the heart of the people who despise it, that a material middle class who know they are it, with their straightened bond of family to control it, is the one thing always human, vital, and worthy it—worth that all monotonously shall repeat it—and from which has always sprung, and all who really look can see it,
> (37) the very best the world can ever know, and everywhere we always need it.

It sounds like a manifesto. In a voice we come to find increasingly familiar, this narrator seems to be letting us in on what they truly stand for. It sounds like a clear theme in a novel where such things eventually become slippery and hard to pin down.

And that is likely the point. Stein's novel requires recognition, first, that this narrator is a construct, that they are unreliable and honest, both self-aware and blind to their own prejudices. This writerly voice equivocates and recreates, as fiction writers do. And while they set out to tell you what it takes to "make" Americans, that promise is kept on their terms, with their limitations. As writing happens, ideas change. In the final chapter, references to democracy, middle-class living, landscape, even marriage all peel away, and only "family living" remains to give meaning to existence for the novel's characters, now all dead. *TMOA* was, as promised, "the History of a Family's Progress." And only in family living, through remembering, do these Americans, Herslands and Dehnings, "go on existing" (1021).

Chapter Four
Lesbian Subtexts: *The (Un)Making of Patriarchy*

HETERO-PATRIARCHY MAY SEEM, at first glance, to be an overarching theme of this novel, as Stein claims it's the story of one family's progress—through grandfathers and grandmothers, parents and children. But, in fact, the devastating failures of heteronormative marriages in *TMOA* starkly contrast with the successes of women to women relationships, romantic, platonic, and familial, and with the mutual support women characters offer one another.

From the very beginning, the narrator *knows* the reader will assume that the stereotypical oppressed woman of the nineteenth and twentieth century has a predictable path already planned for her, one where she is groomed to become a wife from the moment she is born. This would lead inevitably to the trap of an oppressive marriage where said wife is constrained from achieving marital happiness through mutual affection, sex, and love. This plot/plight could typify many a secular, stereotyped "women's novel." And we begin *TMOA* with the promise of this narrative arc, through Julia Dehning:

> And so those who read much in story books surely now can tell what to expect of her, and yet, please reader, remember that this is perhaps not the whole of our story either . . . for I am not ready to take away the character from our Julia . . . so reader, please remember, the future is not certain for her. (16)

Yet the narrator warns us that sweet, sweet Julia, the very image of the ideal, submissive, American woman, the "crude virgin . . . safe in her freedom," is not to be so quickly trusted, for Julia is already suspicious of the heteronormative patriarchy she is born into (15). "[F]or even with her well guarded life she had found the sickened sense that comes with learning that some men do wrong" (20).

In Stein's Paris notebooks where she scribbled much of the brainstormed, first draft of *TMOA*, she riffs on marriage in a passage that doesn't make it into the novel's final draft: "They expect to find in these weak husbands the love and support they had at home and then this springs an eternal tragedy."[1] What does show up in the novel is this: "Every one, then, as I was saying have in them . . . their way of being attracted by women and by men" (271). This distinction does not refer to men being attracted to women, or women being attracted by men, but rather leaves an ambiguous space open for the attraction to exist in multiple realms. It seems clear from these early drafts, and from the novel itself, that Stein was never interested on putting a successful heterosexual marriage on display. She was hell-bent on deconstructing it.

These views against an oppressive heteronormative marriage follow Julia Dehning around, as the narrator discusses her romantic life in an indirect way, hinting constantly at the inevitable failure of marriage—"Loving is alright as a beginning but then there is marrying and that is very different" (73). Women follow a dangerous path when they deviate from prescribed norms of heteropatriarchy, but having lesbian experiences or even tight-knit friendships that give women agency over their own bodies and sexuality are obvious threats to patriarchy, threats to masculine power. The joke's on the hetero men, though, because these women all have "resisting being" within them, and they know how to use it. So, although women in *TMOA* are often described as mild and content, they are nearly always successful at resisting the patriarchal ideals coming at them from all angles (sons, fathers, brothers, husbands).

1. This quote was taken directly from Stein's first written manuscript of *The Making of Americans* (Beinecke Library, Holograph manuscript #1 [YCAL MSS76 Box 40] accessed 1.72019)

These ideals make the way that sexuality is constructed through heteronormative relationships very different for men versus women in the novel. Masculine heterosexuality is presented, often with disgust, as leaving no room for a woman's freedom. The narrator points out: "Loving is good, and the girl has to be pleasing to him, but it needs coaxing, arranging, flattering teasing, urging, a little good tempered irritated forcing, or else the man will forget all about his loving" (74-75). Here the narrator packs women's sexuality into a nice, tightly-packed box of irony. *Woman* becomes *girl*, effectively stripping her sexual agency from her by diminishing her age, demeaning her maturity and stomping out her right to make choices. A woman must present her sexuality to a man in a heterosexual relationship in the correct way, and do it persistently enough to keep his attention, otherwise, "he will forget all about" it.

David Hersland II, for example, bolsters his personal power and sexual dominance through the feelings of superiority he experiences when comparing his success to other men, but his masculine sexual energy doesn't come across in the same way as women's in the text. David has a rather aggressive sexuality-in-practice. "Women could never give him any such feeling to have inside him. If they [women] had power in them, he would brush them away from around him"; but if a woman "held her power" it was due to her "brilliant seductive managing, and so there would not be aroused in him any desire of fighting nor brushing her away" (95). Where Hersland gets to retain his sexual freedom, any woman he desires falls on a double-edged sword. On one side, the woman is allowed to unleash her sexuality in the form of manipulative power over Mr. Hersland, or over men in general. Yet, the other stabby side of the sword condemns her for being sexual and forces her to hide her desire if she is to be socially (or sexually) acceptable. Unfortunately, this depiction of Hersland's sexuality is only one disappointing example of how easily the responsibility for the failures of heteronormativity fall on women's shoulders.

Another vivid example of this failure is in Martha Hersland's romantic experience with a youthful crush that a boy her age develops for her: "One little boy wanted her to do loving . . . but this was not very much of a success for Martha then had a nervous feeling and was not very daring"

(454). Suggesting their lack of relationship success was due to Martha not acting daring enough "to do loving" with this boy places blame on her character and reminds young women of their place and plight. This persistent trope of the double bind women face in choosing either modesty and sexual adventurousness, where both are required of her, teaches boys like the one in this passage that they are in a win-win situation. Only the girl, whose purpose is to please him, can fail.

Martha's subsequent experiences with men do not differ much from this experience with the young boy. Martha's husband Phillip Redfern, for example, is at first infatuated with her; their relationship lasts three years before they marry. Soon after, however, Redfern realizes that all of Martha's personality "proved sufficiently inadequate to his needs" (477). She was everything, but not for long and not for him. When Redfern becomes a professor of philosophy, he soon leaves Martha for the reticent Miss Dounor, who has been in a relationship with Miss Charles, the dean of the college. Miss Charles, dismayed at Redfern's interference, tells Martha (not Phillip) that it's her job to keep her husband in line (even as he is *cheating* on her) in order to protect Miss Dounor's reputation. "'He is dishonorable, all his action is deceit,' she [Martha] said to herself again and again but she found no comfort in this thought" (484). The narrative then suggests that while Phillip possesses the power of charm and masculine privilege, Martha becomes only, dangerously, a woman out for vengeance. "Redfern was a man too much on guard to fear surprise and with all his experience too ignorant of women's ways to see danger where danger really lay" (484).

Redfern, earlier described as a champion for women, is finally a cheater "gone altogether wrong," a man "always wronging every one" (493). But Martha—that Martha!—ends up "studying and striving and travelling and working" when she is out of her marriage to Phillip (517). From the time Martha sees a man hit a woman with an umbrella in her childhood, she wants to become an educated woman, one who understands why men and women act the way they do. Although Martha's marriage to Redfern ends as a complete failure for him, his reputation in ruins, Martha goes on to better things than Redfern, fulfilling the feminist prophecy that began with that umbrella. And, thus, a marriage is narratively deconstructed with the woman not only surviving, but thriving.

The marriage at the center of the plot (such as it is), the one that joins the novel's two central families, is the one between Alfred Hersland and the woman who could be characterized as the ultimate resisting being, Julia Dehning. We learn, after many dark hints, that this union doesn't last. While early on Julia "liked it a little then" their marriage "went on to come to be quite soon a beginning of a long ending, a long dividing of themselves from living with each other any more in being in living" (758). Alfred and Julia's marriage unravels more slowly across the novel than most of the other relationships, over mountains of repetition, through valleys of fading romance. There is barely any sign of attraction, despite their having two children together.

Having married Alfred at a young age, encouraged by her mother and her storybooks to marry, Julia is only later able to cultivate friendships with a large group of people, one of them being David Hersland, once her brother in law (775). Having gained her independence, Julia almost marries again, with William Beckling, but Beckling has a chronic illness and does not want to burden Julia with it. Julia lives a long life full of friendships (so many names!) and time with her two children. Alfred, in stereotypically toxic-masculine fashion, does not see his children often, nor does he have any other children after remarrying—to Minnie Mason. In opposition to marriage plot of the stereotypical women's novel, Julia's marriage, which appears at first to be the focal point of the novel, ends long before the novel's resolution—and her happily-ever-after, like Martha's, clearly comes after the marriage ends.

There is only a single central male character whose sexual orientation and romantic life are completely ambiguous, thus challenging the heterosexual norm. Coincidentally, David Hersland III, reflective and thoughtful, is often described in his section as level-headed. The narrator points out repeatedly in multiple variations that David, "would have liked all of his living to feel beauty in any kind there is of women" (811). It is not clear whether David is incapable of feeling beauty in any kind of woman, or if he just hasn't met a woman he can fall in love with. Either way, this David acts as a contrasting figure to his father and many of the other aggressively heterosexual males in the novel.

What does the narrative's long silence about his sexuality or romantic history do to the perception of David and the question of his identity? What does it do to the concept of a married and successful man? David, the novel's central masculine character, does not fulfill the stereotypical expectations of his father and of American culture more broadly—making money, marrying a woman, then expecting her to take care of him until he dies. David is pretty clear on everything in life except women: "he was pretty completely wanting to be needing to be feeling that any woman that could ever be existing was in some way a really beautiful thing" (873). Then, later, "Certainly he was not completely wanting to be seeing any woman who is existing" (923). He's not sure he wants to be with women, let alone take "ownership" of a woman like many of the male characters surrounding him, though he does briefly have a love interest with feminine pronouns. Then he dies.

The power dynamic the novel depicts in these heterosexual relationships differs sharply in platonic, familial, and romantic relationships between women. Relationships between two women tend to work out even when the relationship has been put under immense strain, and sometimes these relationships occur as a result of a heteronormative marriage falling apart.

When Mrs. Hersland lives near the Shilling sisters, we find that each one of the three women has an "emptiness" in them, a "hole" that ought to be filled. "It will never be known about them whether they had been made so from the beginning, whether something had been left out in each one of them . . . that should have been inside them" (91). The narrator continues:

> And so one could not come to any certain judgement of them, one could never be so sure about them, that they had something queer inside them . . . It is easy to see how this puzzling quality of them would awaken in Mrs. Hersland who was almost always now with them, the always possible most important feeling that was quiet until then inside her. (91-92)

Could this most important feeling lying dormant within Mrs. Hersland until now be possibly, maybe, I don't know, queerness? While she had "a very little such [important] feeling with her husband when she was first married to him" she found "a little more in her feeling with the Shilling family in her hotel living." But it was "strongest in her" with "Madeleine Wyman who was for her the one who in all her living was the one whom she had power over" (181).

Perhaps the most intriguingly queer representation in the novel is in the frequent repetition of Mabel and Mary's story. When Mary, a strong and confident single woman, becomes pregnant, jeopardizing her respectable reputation, her good friend Mabel stays by her. Six months into her pregnancy, Mary miscarries, so Mabel takes care of Mary in her despair. Mary can't explain her feelings to Mabel, but she is apparently falling in love with her, idolizing her with the repeated refrain, "angel Mabel, Mabel is an angel." The narrator tells us that, "Mabel was everything she wanted and that was enough for her feeling," (252) but that Mary "always wanted [Mabel] more than Mabel wanted her" (253). The unexplainable love Mary has for Mabel, a love she has to keep completely secret and safe inside of her, is a writer's resistance to patriarchy. Queer folks have always existed, and existence is not resistance, it's a human right. However, the fact that the novel features this story, retelling it matter-of-factly, from several angles, is an act of resistance. Certainly coming from a woman writer of the time period, it is an overt challenge to the heteropatriarchal order.

And the honesty of the story's ending is breathtaking: "Mabel Linker had her lover, Mary found ingratitude then in her, things got so that they could no longer live together" (252). Mary's story is familiar: painfully navigating her sexuality and her feelings for Mabel, in the end, she loses the woman she loves to a heterosexual relationship, one that represents what Mary wishes she could nurture with Mabel. As Mary tries desperately to stop Mabel's marriage to a younger man, their relationship crumbles. Mary is eventually set to marry the father of the child she lost. Perhaps it's an act of love, but more likely it's a full submergence of her own emotions, a trade-off to live a more acceptable life. The two women can't keep away from one another, though, and the novel can't let them go—so they come back to dressmaking and form a successful business together. The novel allows them a space, regardless of their husbands, to remain faithfully close, providing steady support in one another's lives, as the women of *TMOA* do.

And that's a wrap! Or, an un-wrap, of the patriarchal rules that governed the lives of so many artists of the nineteenth and early twentieth centuries, weaved through individual characters' stories in Stein's thick novel. Today, when it is not (quite) so necessary to hide what makes us who they are, we may find ourselves relating to the Mables and Marys, the Young Davids, the Mrs. Herslands and the Julias of *TMOA*. We discover courage and resistance in them, as they explore their uncertainty about existing within the parameters of the worlds they negotiate. Many heard that same reassuring voice while reading Stein's work at a time when she walked the streets of Paris. Stein appeared on the literary scene ready to kick the "normal" relationships aggrandized in romantic novels out the door. And she did—to the best of her ability—within the parameters she felt safe adhering to in a society not yet ready for "brother singulars" and folks with "a little queerness" in them.

Part Three:
Summary

We should note immediately that "Summary" is loosely stated here. In this novel very often *nothing happens*, as many readers have famously pointed out. Plot disappears, and experiments with language—words, sentences, sounds, even placements on the page—take over. It is a Gertrude Stein novel after all.

But it helped us as we read to keep track of the family at the (unstable) center of the novel. You will probably want to keep referencing our "Cast of Characters" and "Family Tree." For much of the first half of the book, following their story is fairly simple; we include more extensive plot summary for these early pages. The plot, such as it is, however, unravels slowly, until in the final pages the family is centered and decentered repeatedly, pretty much lost in a blur of words and the ruminations of a narrator who goes from being the novel's main character to disappearing along with the others. Here, summary becomes nearly impossible, so we do what we can.

In the quotes that follow, we have maintained the idiosyncratic spelling of Stein's original texts—and the Dalkey Archive Essential edition—without notation, including the words "realising," "sombre," "generalisation," the divided "every one," and the frequent lack of apostrophes.

Cast of Characters

THE NARRATOR | A genderless, omniscient character set on categorizing types of being and the natures of people. They are enamored with the endless, cyclical repetition of people's behaviors, with ideas and psychological constructs, with the rich and the poor, society women, college girls, nannies, seamstresses, and maids, and they aren't afraid to share their thoughts with the reader while openly engaging in novel writing.

The Dehnings

STRONG GRANDMOTHER #2 | Mother to Henry, this first Julia was strong to die and leave her children (4).

GOOD ORDINARY HUSBAND | Also known as Henry (formerly Herman), he was a decent, honest, hardworking man, married to Strong Grandmother #2.

HENRY DEHNING | Father to Julia, George, and Hortense, Henry is a generous and kind natured man who is fond of his wife, Jenny, and of his children whom he respects, though he isn't afraid to remind them of how good they have it because of him.

JENNY DEHNING | Married to Henry Dehning, the mother of Julia, George, and Hortense. Particular in her taste and style, Jenny is a loud voiced, pleasant looking heavy woman but "one whom one might like better the more one saw her less" (14).

SWEET GRANDMOTHER #4 | Mother to Jenny, she was "strong to suffer" with her children (4).

JULIA DEHNING | Early in the novel, she is a bright, ambitious and energetic 18-year-old who resembles her mother and is named for her grandmother. She is described as a strong domineering crude virgin as well as hopeless romantic raised and educated in the ways of patriarchy and privilege. She tends to disregard her gut feeling when something feels wrong, and her life takes unexpected turns as the novel progresses.

GEORGE DEHNING | An athletic, cheerful and hopeful 14-year-old when we first meet him, he is brother to Julia and Hortense.

HORTENSE DEHNING | Sister to Julia and George, Hortense is enamored with her big brother and sister. At ten, when we first meet her, she views them with a "loyal upgazing sweetness."

The Herslands

STRONG GRANDMOTHER #1 | Mother of David Hersland, also named Martha, she is "strong to bear and lead her children" from the Old World to a better life in America (4); she teaches her family how to be self-sufficient and make their own wealth; married to David "The Butcher" Hersland.

DAVID "THE BUTCHER" HERSLAND | Also known as DAVID HERSLAND I, he is a small, gentle, pleasant looking family man with blue eyes and "a lightish colored beard" who marries Strong Grandmother #1. Religion is important to him; he finds comfort in the familiar, which gives him trouble when his family sets out to emigrate.

THE GLUTTON | One of the seven children that Strong Grandmother #1 and David Hersland produce. He is the only one spoiled by his mother; he dies relatively young leaving a wife and children.

OLDER MARTHA HERSLAND | Married to a "soggy" husband (for the "very soggy passion in him"), she is sister to David Hersland II. She is not particularly strong or weak, nor is she pleasing or not pleasing. She pursues "the right way to do in the business of living" and is a reliable judge of character.

DAVID HERSLAND II | A large man with small, piercing eyes and gray hair and thick eyebrows, he is a son of David I and Strong Grandmother #1 and the father of the family at the center of the novel. He is generally respected and listened to, but his children find him strange. He has a temper, especially when he finds himself losing control of his wife or children.

FANNY HISSON HERSLAND | Marries David Hersland II and becomes the mother of the family at the center of the novel. She surrounds herself with people she believes are lesser than her—to give herself "an important feeling." This becomes especially true after her independent children no longer need her. She dies rather young, when her children are in their teens.

MARTHA HERSLAND | Oldest child and daughter of Fanny and David, she is "a blond good-looking young woman full of moral purpose and educational desires," yet is described as not very interesting and easily forgotten. Named for her aunt and grandmother, she is haunted by her observations of gendered power structures from a young age, which causes her to go to college to understand more about men, women, and the world she lives in.

ALFRED HERSLAND | The tall, handsome, well dressed son of Fanny and

David, he has blond hair which he daringly parts down the middle. He later marries Julia Dehning, though her family initially (and subsequently) doesn't like him for reasons they can't at first put their finger on, but it may have something to do with his education and knowledge of art and music. We come to discover that Alfred is not an entirely honest man.

"YOUNG" DAVID HERSLAND III | Younger son of Fanny and David Hersland II, he is a good listener and advice-giver with many friends and a hungry curiosity about the people and the world around him. He understands the fragility of life, having been born after two siblings who died. Surrounded by anger in his "younger living," David makes a conscious effort not to let anger dictate his life. Eventually, unexpectedly, takes over as the narrative focus of the novel.

PHILLIP REDFERN | Husband of Martha Hersland, he sees himself as a champion of "liberty, equality, opportunity, beauty, feeling, for all women," but, in reality, that couldn't be farther from the truth. He lacks self-awareness, and soon his high opinion of himself becomes obviously misguided. Though many see him as intelligent, they also see him as a liar, a cheater, and a weak and dishonorable man.

GOOD GRANDMOTHER #3 | Never has a name, as far as we can tell, but she is "strong to weep, and to be sad and weary with her children" (4). She is mother to Fanny Hisson Hersland and her happy Hisson siblings, and was said to have wept all of the sadness out of her children, who then go on to live contented lives.

RELIGIOUS HUSBAND | A man who finds his importance in religion, he marries Good Grandmother #3 and is father to Fanny Hisson.

Other Characters

The Shillings, together, are summed up as "just ordinary stupid enough women like millions of them" who are also "queer" with "big doughy empty heads"; they seem essentially unimportant, yet they take up a lot of narrative space throughout the middle sections of the novel.

MRS. SHILLING | Mother to Sophie and Pauline.

SOPHIE SHILLING | The fatter of the two Shilling sisters, she is "afraid of the other because it would hurt more if pins were stuck into her."

PAULINE SHILLING | The thinner of the two Shilling sisters.

MR. JAMESON | A seemingly pleasant 35-year-old man who turns out to have an unhealthy, intimate attachment to Julia Dehning. He often rode his horse with Julia, much to Mrs. Jameson's dismay.

MR. RICHARDSON | "a tall thin blonde man" living in a small house in Gossols. He finds his importance in religion and has two children named Eddy and Lilly.

ANNA | Young and beautiful daughter of an unnamed foreign dressmaker who works constantly, (including for the Herslands), to support her children. She has two younger sisters, Cora and Bertha, and a father who is never clearly identified.

MADELEINE WYMAN | A governess for the Hersland family, Madeleine has a peculiar influence on Fanny and a relationship with her, the nature of which is never made quite clear but seems central to Fanny's life. In spite of her later marriage to John Summers, she continues to work for the Herslands who double her wages and gift her an elaborate dress made by Mary and Mabel.

OTHER WYMANS | Madeleine's siblings, Louise and Frank and Helen, and their long-lived mother, Mrs. Wyman

JOHN SUMMERS | Marries Madeleine Wyman and adopts a little girl only to send her back because Madeleine does not want a child along while they travel. They are very happy together until he dies of an unknown illness.

MARY MAXWORTHING | A dressmaker for Mrs. Hersland in Gossols, Mary is full of ambition and values her freedom. She miscarries a baby she conceives out of wedlock, during which she becomes attached to her friend and business partner, Mabel.

MABEL LINKER | The seemingly aloof friend of Mary who helps her through her miscarriage, Mabel is a talented dressmaker, Mary's business partner and longtime companion.

LILLIAN ROSENHAGEN | An anxious dressmaker for the Herslands, she is large, tall, and black-haired; "a stupid woman" who "never said anything"; a "spinster," she has a mother who does some cleaning and cooking and a sister named Cecilia.

CECILIA ROSENHAGEN | Similar to Lillian but lacks her sewing skills and is a spinster by nature rather than by circumstance.

MARTHA, "THE FOREIGN WOMAN" | A governess for the Herslands, she is a musician who comes to the states with her younger sister to help her become a teacher; Martha doesn't enjoy America and means to go back to Europe but only gets as far as Ohio, where she spends the rest of her days.

HANNAH CHARLES | Dean of Farnham College, she introduces her protégée Miss Dounor to Phillip Redfern; she forces Martha to confront Phillip's infidelity when people start to talk.

CORA DOUNOR | Friend to Miss Charles, Cora is a quiet, intellectual woman who enters into an affair with Phillip Redfern, upsetting Hannah Charles.

WILLIAM BECKLING | Possibly would have become Julia's second husband but decides not to marry because of his illness.

MINNIE MASON | Alfred's second wife who has been in love three times and married twice.

More Minor Characters

OLGA | The sister of "Martha, The Foreign Woman"; becomes a teacher in Gossols; never visits her sister because she is afraid of her; dies a spinster.

MR. ARRAGON | Music teacher of Alfred, who is very fond of him.

"BLONDE LITTLE WOMAN" WITH CURLS | For a paragraph, and several times after, the narrator focuses on one particular servant who can't cook or clean, but stays a while with the Herslands; she lies constantly.

TALL BLOND WOMAN WITH NO QUEERNESS | Also a governess to the Herlands; marries a baker. She is never important to the children, but Mr. Hersland visits her at the bakery even after she leaves them.

JOHNSON, FRANK HACKART, MARY HELBING, SARAH SANDS, MELANCTHA | Mentioned as being similar to Redfern in that they are "self-deceived"; they think of themselves one way, while the rest of society views them differently (and not in a good way).

THE IMMORAL FATHER AND HIS DAUGHTER, EDITH | In a narrative interlude, she calls her father out for abusing her and rejects him.

THE FATHER AND HIS BUG-COLLECTING SON | In another repeated narrative interlude, this father convinces his son that killing insects is wrong, but later gifts a beautiful moth, dead and pinned, to his now confused son.

AUNT HILDA | Helps the Baltimore branch of the Hersland family dissuade Alfred from marrying his first love.

PAT MOORE | A friend of Alfred Hersland who introduces Alfred to his second wife, Minnie Mason, as well as to James Flint, the clothing manufacturer, and Mackinly Young, the musician.

IDA THE SCHOOLTEACHER | Ida is sister to Alfred's governess Olga; both Alfred and Mr. Arragon like Ida at first, but it turns out she is "a queer one" and "a stupid resisting, stagnant, dull fairly sensible one" with a "nervous kind of crazy kind of asking every one to be a lover to her."

THE HENRYS | Including siblings James, Rose, and Carrie, the Henrys encounter the Herslands through the theater and often eat dinner with them. James Henry later commits suicide.

ADOLPH DEHNING | Henry Dehning's brother.

HARRY BRENNER AND JOHN DAVIDSON | former boyfriends of Martha Hersland.

FRIENDS OF YOUNG ALFRED | The three Banks boys, Louis Champion, Frank and Will Roddy, the four Fisher children and the four Henrys.

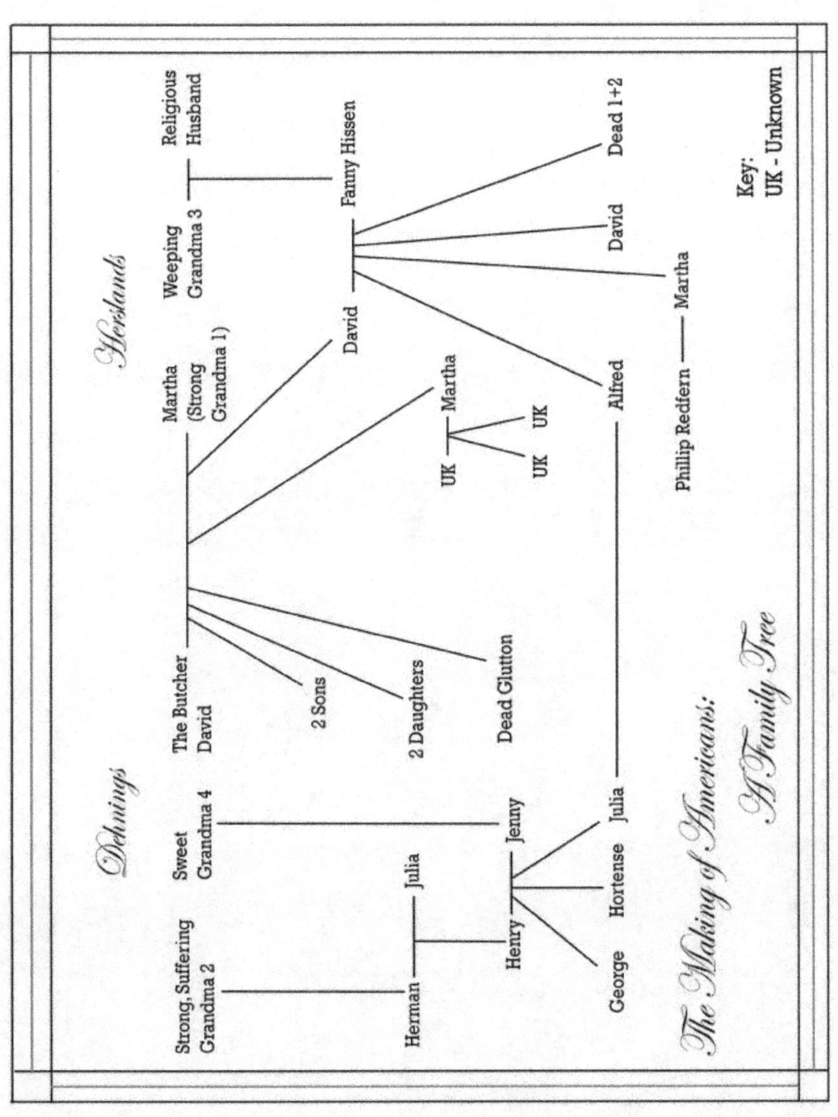

Image by Emma Hargreaves and Maia Labrie

Epigraph

MUCH HAS BEEN made of this epigraph in which "an angry man" drags his father "along the ground through his own orchard"; it's a three-line story, based on an Aristotelian reflection,[1] that calls our attention to generational difference, inherited temperaments, family dynamics and other themes of the narrative to follow, but it is also enigmatic. The "groaning old man" insists that his son: "Stop, I did not drag my father beyond this tree" (3).

Is the dragging a tradition, then? Is the anger inherited? And more to the point, who are these people? The novel offers a brief explanation in the second paragraph, initiating a refrain that will later become a recurrent and obsessive focus: "It is hard living down the tempers we are born with" (3). Apparently, we all struggle throughout our lives with what the narrator later calls "our bottom natures," until we realize that many of our "sins" are harmless and "give a charm to any character, and so our struggle with them dies away."

Critics and Stein admirers often cite this epigraph, we suspect because it is such a strong image, so specific and visual, in a text with few moments

1. Deborah Mix explains the relationship of Stein's father-dragging son and Aristotle's in her *A Vocabulary of Thinking: Gertrude Stein and Contemporary North American Women's Innnovative Writing* (U of Iowa, 2007) p. 130–131.

like it. The operatic adaptation of the novel uses it extensively.[2] But be forewarned: if you hold onto that father-dragging son and wait for him to reappear in the novel, you will be disappointed.

2. An opera by Anthony Gatto, "The Making of Americans" premiered at the Walker Art Center in Minneapolis in December 2008.

Part One

[THE DEHNINGS AND THE HERSLANDS]

Pages 1–12 | The narrative "I" commands the novel's first lines, noting what "a rare privilege" it is to be a "real American," meaning, we come to see, the descendants of immigrants who only have to trace back three generations to know their complete history (3).

We begin with some history of the immigrant American families we will follow through the novel. In the first pages, we find out that several women were "strong to bear many children" (4). These women are placed center stage and described, one by one, as (#1) being strong to bear and lead their children, (#2) to die and leave them, (#3) to weep, be sad with and weary with them, and (#4) to suffer with them. The women and the generations after them come together as the characters that make up our main families, the Dehnings and Herslands.

Following these introductory notes, the narrator assertively reenters the text in a way that will become familiar. They address the reader directly and inclusively, using "our" and "we" repeatedly. We introduce this narrator in Part 2, Chapter 1, so you can turn there for more information about them, but for now you should know that we use "they/them" throughout when discussing the narrator, because they are determinedly not gendered. Here they suggest that memories are never comparable to the moment

in time when things actually occur occurred. Because memories of our youth continue to be vivid, **"We, living now, are always to ourselves young men**
(4) **and women."** They also compare the feeling of growing old to "a horrid losing-self feeling" like dropping off to sleep.

After the narrative intrusion and a quick reference to those strong grandmothers and to one of their (good-enough ordinary) husbands, we meet Henry Dehning as an older man. The son and caregiver to that ordinary husband and Strong Grandmother #2, Henry is found observing his children with the same sense of bewilderment that his dying father had expressed in conversations with him. Like his father, Henry has "got nothing now really to do with [his children's] new kinds of ways of living" (7). And, with that, the story skips over most of Henry's life, as well as that of his ordinary father—as yet unnamed, though we discover later that he, too, is named Henry (sometimes Herman), and his wife (the strong grandmother who dies and leaves her children) is Julia (see *Characters*).

At this narrative moment, the younger Henry is an aging father "always very full of such talking"; he is a rich man, and he tells his own children (for several pages) that he worked hard so they could have a comfortable, pleasant life (8). He insists that his children have it much easier than he did because of what he accomplished. "[Y]ou have no idea what an easy time you children have nowadays just doing nothing," he tells them (9). This is, obviously, a familiar generational sentiment, and the repetition of it reinforces that point. The Dehning family's generational difference is not bitter angry or unpleasant, but rather "a cheerful challenge" (10). Henry **"liked it and [his children] liked it too with him, to fight strongly against him in the everlasting struggle of conscious unproved power in the young against**
(10) **dogmatic pride in having done it, of the old ones"**

Pages 12–22 | The novel then introduces Henry's children—Julia, George, and Hortense—who Henry believes his wife, Jenny, has spoiled. He tells his children (repeatedly we suspect) about coming to America with his brother, just the two of them from their family of ten children. He reminds his children that *his* mother (again, Julia, Strong Grandmother #2) was nearly perfect, and, by comparison, they won't amount to much of anything: "you don't any of you children look much like her" (11). Like his father before him he distrusts their "new fangled notions" and tells them he will just have to wait around to see what they can do with their "new world ideals." Because of their father's devotion to making money, the children live a "contented joyous" family life in a very nice home in Bridgepoint, which critics of *TMOA* have noted is inspired by Baltimore, Maryland (12).

After a quick introduction to Mrs. Dehning/Jenny, "the quintessence of loud-voiced good-looking prosperity," the story shifts to their daughter and oldest child, Julia, named for her grandmother (14). Julia is in the prime of her American girlhood, "now just eighteen and she showed in all its vigor, the self satisfied crude domineering American girlhood that was strong inside her." (15) The text repeatedly references her "crude virginity" and the safety she finds in her liberty and freedom. So, clearly, the time has come for Julia to find a husband and get married, as the ideal nineteenth-century American woman, beautiful, well-mannered, rich and proper, must do.

When the narrator reenters the text to discuss Julia here, they take on a new tone, addressing the reader directly in the style of the romantic novels of the eighteenth and nineteenth centuries. "Reader," they warn, "please remember, the future is not yet certain for her" (16). In other words, don't expect some fairytale rubbish or happily-ever-after. Then the narrative voice takes a quick one-page detour into a discussion of washing, as it has to do with George, the middle child, who was "strong in sport and washing" (16). Taking the story down a notch from romance and fairy tales to the absolutely mundane, they point out that people across histories and cultures have always been critical of each other's ways of washing. The washing discussion draws out some redundancies in human nature, but it also plays for humor, concluding, "Yes it certainly is all very funny, and so we come back to talk more about George Dehning" (17). And that transition, to us, is funnier still.

After the narrator finishes this detour, the story circles back to the omniscient third person and to the Dehnings, but specifically to George, the middle child. He is described as athletic, fair, and cheery, but like most teenage boys at fourteen he does not have much sense in him. Morally sound and hopeful, George expresses his goodness through the time he spends with his younger sister, Hortense, just ten years old. For her part, she adores her brother with a "loyal upgazing sweetness" (19). Because their mother is engaged in the important matter of "the marrying of Julia," Hortense is "left much to her brother and to the governess" (19).

Julia is centered as special to the whole family. Both of her siblings look up to her, and her parents adore her. Her virginity is, again, noted frequently, perhaps ironically, to call out this ridiculous pre-modernist value. For example, the narrator notes: **"It was not for nothing she was a crude**
(19) **domineering virgin."** Despite her feminine perfection, Julia, "ambitious for passion and . . . a strain of romance," has trouble finding the perfect man. There is a foreboding aside about how the good men that surrounded her in her family left her, "an impetuous woman," unprepared to negotiate "a world of passions" (20). Instead, "they only made a sane and moral background on which she in her later life could learn to lean" (20).

In another brief aside, Julia definitely appears to have experienced queer encounters in finishing school where "she became acquainted with that dubious character, the adventuress, the type to be found always in all kinds of places, a character eternally attractive in its mystery and daring, and always able to attach unto itself the most intelligent and honest of its comrades and introduce them to queer vices" (21). So, in many ways beyond piano playing and lessons [wink, wink], finishing school prepared her "to be a woman" (21).

So there is young Julia, "full of courage and experience and wisdom," ready to conquer all the world (21). But there's one more menacing moment, when she gets involved in what she thinks is a platonic relationship with Jameson, "a pleasant man of thirty five or thereabouts," who just happens to show up wherever she rides her horse. When she notices "Mrs. Jameson frown[ing] on her in anger," Julia "understood at last and did not ride with him again" (22).

Pages 22–33 | Later, Julia's cousin brings his friend, Alfred Hersland, over to the house, and Alfred makes her "heart beat with surprise." That, my friends, is true romance. Cue another lecture from the narrator, who wants us to understand that, for a young woman, "singularity" can be a dangerous thing. While the thrust of this lesson is a bit tough to follow, it has something to do with the "bourgeois mind" and its "fervor for diversity," how middle-class Americans crave singularity "within the limits of conventional respectability." However, a young woman, especially a marriageable one, needs to be careful not to expose herself as too different from those around her. The narrator addresses men who are singular, the "Brother Singulars," a "misplaced generation" subject to constant disapproval, with a tendency to leave America and "fly to the kindly comfort of an older world" (23). Using an inclusive American "we," the narrator laments that singularity is "yet an unknown product with us." Apparently, **"It takes time to make queer people and to have others who can know it"** and the U.S. doesn't yet have the goods. (23)

Alfred, who is "tall and well dressed and sufficiently good looking," and part of "a Western family" of Herslands, is "a poor thing" to the Brother Singulars, "even hardly then our own" (23). He comes to college in Bridgepoint, his mother's hometown, to practice law and make his own money (later we will discover that he is the grandson of the Grandmother #1, who was strong to bear and lead many children). Like Julia, he has a very successful father. His is in Gossols (referencing Stein's childhood home of Oakland, California), so Alfred has to leave there and set out on his own to make his own life.

Alfred's love for art appeals to Julia, who apparently has always longed to learn about art, especially since being "out of doors with men was soiled . . . by the grossness of the Jamesons" (23). This love of art, of playing the piano and parting his hair in the middle, puts Alfred's masculinity under scrutiny for Julia's male cousins and uncles. While Julia decides quickly that she and Alfred will live their "lives together, always learning things and doing things, good things they will be for us whatever other people may think or say" (24), the rest of the family needs some convincing. So, the next six pages record the long and slow process of convincing her father "to let her some time get married to him" (29).

Though the entire family shares the assumption that Julia belongs to her father, and, of course, that she requires his approval to marry, the

passages that describe their back-and-forth iterations record a loving, mutually respectful exchange. Henry tries "it's not me, it's your mother," and Julia refocuses him: "She would be the same about anybody that I would want" (27). Julia works to convince her father that just because Alfred is different from him doesn't make him bad for her. Though she values Henry's wise judgments and his understanding, Julia recognizes that her father is "of the old generation" and "surely must fail to see the meanings in the unaccustomed" (26). It is hard for Julia "to have to always begin over every time she started to talk about it with her father," but she still loves the struggle with him. "**They loved and admired and respected each**
(28) **other very much this daughter and her father.**"

The narrative then leads the reader through a final conversation between Julia and her father while they are out walking together. Henry tells his daughter not to make a decision about marrying Alfred until they return to town after their summer away in their country home. Julia agrees not to see Alfred until then, but finds that time away from him doesn't change her mind. "And so at last, filled full with faith and hope and fine new joy she went back to her busy city life, strong in the passion of her eager young imagining" (30). After a brief interlude about home decorating styles in Paris, London and Bridgepoint, "At last it was agreed that these two young people should become engaged" (30).

As the novel continues, a year passes, and Julia is even more in love with Alfred than she was when they first met. They are now engaged, but she recognizes that "dimly, somewhere, in her head and heart now there was sometimes a vague dread," recalling for readers the foreboding moments of her life up to this point. Something, we sense, is wrong here. Julia's dread, the narrative notes, "comes of ignorance and a beginning wisdom," along with a growing distrust that she can't confront directly (31).

There follows a fascinating detour, a discussion of "story-books," and how, as we age, we understand that there was wisdom "that we have been spending our lives winning" in those very books. This proves, for the narrator, that "no young people can learn wisdom from the talking of the older ones around them" if they can't even learn it from books where "it is all made lifelike, real and interesting for them." Though this passage is full

of strong opinion and addressed toward an implied (well read) reader, the narrator isn't revealed until the "us" in the final line: they are among the story tellers. "**Yes from their fathers' and their mothers' living they can get some wisdom, yes supply them with a tradition by your lives, you grown men and women, and for the rest let them come to us for their teaching.**" Authors are obviously (31)
the proper folks for young people to seek knowledge from. Obviously.

"But now we come back to Julia Dehning." These abrupt transitions always strike us as funny. Weren't we talking about Julia all along? This segue also marks the first appearance of "As I was saying," a refrain we took as the title for this book because it eventually, and persistently, becomes *TMOA*'s signature phrase (31).

Julia is naive, we learn, because she doesn't believe the men in her world could be as bad as the men she's heard about in stories. Yet, as Jenny excitedly begins wedding preparations, Julia quietly harbors doubts about marrying Alfred. The text suggests she is pondering over her own ideals, trying to see how they match up with Alfred's (32).

Julia's ideals concretely take the shape of domestic arrangements, which are discussed in Bridezilla-level detail. We learn that the house that Julia and Alfred are furnishing is "a small edition of her mother's," but much less comfortable, with "no solid warm substantial riches" (33). The narrator has strong opinions about home decorating (and washing), and reminds us that modernism looms on the horizon, with the impending "passion for the simple line and toned green burlap on the wall and wooden panelling all classic and severe." But that's still twenty years away, and though Julia prefers simplicity, her mother brings "that natural sense for gilding and all kinds of paint and complicated decoration" (33). This mother-daughter conflict is less charming and loving than the father-daughter exchange. Jenny is disgusted with her daughter's taste; she sneers at it, and then is "beaten back and overborne" by "the hardness of unconsidering disregard" that Julia meets her with (32).

Still, Julia's parents are proud of her for all that she's accomplished (she's getting married, after all), little Hortense worships her and George admires her, so "these were brilliant days for Julia" (34). In the midst of these domestic concerns, though, Julia's doubts about her future husband

persist: **"But somehow, a little, he was there in her as an unknown power that**
(34) **might attack her."** Strong words, indeed. This "vague distrust" turns "a little
sharper" when Alfred solicits Julia's complicity. He exults that his big ideas
and risky ventures will be easier to subsidize when everyone associates
him with Julia's successful, reliable father. Not yet, he says, but later when
they are married he will exploit that association, he implies. She pulls
back, and Alfred reassures her that he didn't mean anything by this reference to her father's money—and adds that she can't say anything to her
father because her loyalty is now to her soon-to-be husband. With that,
Julia focuses on the promise of their future together, and "Hersland was
safe, though very simply now, he often made for her that sharp uncertain
feeling more dreadful and more clear before her" (35). Her doubts keep
returning as the wedding approaches: **"But now she had to think that it was
all, as it had a little sounded, good and best. She had to think is so else how could
she marry him, and how could she not marry him. She had to marry him, and so**
(36) **she had to think it so, and she would think it so, and did."**

At the end of this section "the actual marrying was done" and "their lives together . . . was at last begun." A bit short of happily-ever-after, certainly, and the past tense, the passive construction, and the plural "lives" might have a lot to say about the future of this couple.

[THE HERSLAND PARENTS]

Pages 36–37 | This section begins with one of our favorite passages of
the novel, one that critics (and the two of us) have spent a lot of time
discussing. It appears to be a revelation from a very vulnerable author
directly addressing her readers, and many readers want it to be so—direct
access to Gertrude Stein! Look, she describes her process, writing down
"a little each day here on my scraps of paper," this "scribbled and dirty
and lined paper;" she famously defines this work as **"not just an ordinary
kind of a novel with a plot and conversations to amuse you, but a record of a**
(36) **decent family progress."** There's a full page of revelations about what she is
doing and why, directed right at us, *her readers*! We observe her basking in

her commitment to portraying ordinary people in a "simple middle class monotonous tradition," because, well, it's just the best:

> Middle-class, middle-class, I know no one of my friends who will admit it, one can find no one among you all to belong to it, I know that here we are to be democratic and aristocratic and not have it, for middle class is sordid material unillusioned unaspiring and always monotonous for it is always there and to be always repeated, and yet I am strong, and I am right, and I know it, and I say to you and you are to listen to it, yes here in the heart of the people who despise it, that a material middle class who know they are it, with their straightened bond of family to control it, is the one thing always human, vital, and worthy it—worth that all monotonously shall repeat it—and from which has always sprung, and all who really look can see it, the very best the world can ever know, and everywhere we always need it. (37)

I mean, it sounds like Gertrude. And she needs us to "love, please, this history of this decent family's progress" (34).

Oh, but it's not that easy. And we insist that she, our author-function "Gertrude Stein," is not that artless. First, there's the idea of the reader, imagined into existence while the narrator "truly never feel[s] it that there ever can be for me any such a creature" (36). Once conjured, though, they address that creature: "anyhow reader, bear in your mind—will there be for me every any such a creature—what I have said always before to you." (36) The ever-assertive narrator goes on, metafictionally, delivering the important points about this task in front of us. One, this is no ordinary novel, even when its subject is "ordinary kind of families, histories" (37). Two, I know you readers don't exist (that dirty paper is "really to be to me always my receiver"). But, given that you're what I have, I'm going to ask you to be patient "while I hasten slowly forwards." And it will seem slow, because the work here is to depict "ordinary middle class existence, in simple, firm ordinary middle class traditions" (37).

This passage is really quite inventive in its invocation of the process of writing where it bumps up against the idea of reading. It is also a warning. Fasten your seat belts, we're being told. I've tried to help you understand that this novel is a story of "decent family progress," a middle-class family, an American one. I've given you plot, characters, and conversations up to this point. Now we're going somewhere else together. The style of the novel begins to shift.

Let the serious repetition begin.

Pages 37–48 | And now we head West to become acquainted with the Herslands. David Hersland, Alfred's father, made his money (and a lot of it) in this new country, and at this point (the "present," when Alfred and Julia are marrying) had lived in Gossols for more than twenty years. He married his wife in Bridgepoint but moved with her to Gossols where their five children were born. Only three are still living: Martha, Alfred, and David. The other two died young. This information is presented over and over as something of an anchoring device the rest of the way through the novel.

But this present moment is not a good one for the Herslands. Their mother "was already now a little ailing, the father had no longer his old strength for living, Martha had come back out of her trouble to them [more on that later], Alfred had gone away and left them, David was very soon to follow him" (37). This contrasts with their years of joy in a country house, "an old place left over from the days when Gossols was just beginning" (38). The narrator notes here, and continues to repeat throughout the novel, that this "large wooden house" with a rail fence on ten acres of land "was not in the part of Gossols where the other rich people mostly were living." Much is made, too, of the Hersland children's idyllic youth here among vegetable gardens, fruit trees, vast unkempt lawns, and a hedge of roses that others from Gossols came to pick from. **"It was fun all the things**
(39) **that happened all the year there then."**

The text then returns to those grandmothers we started with thirty pages ago. Martha, Grandmother #1, the one who is "strong to bear many children and always after was very strong to lead them" (39), was mother to David Hersland II, the father here in Gossols. Her back was strong and straight even in her old age; she was a leader who helped her family migrate from the old world to the new one, and "there they learned through her and by themselves, almost every one of them, how to make for themselves each one a sufficient fortune" (39).

Her husband, however, was not so much a leader. Grandfather David "The Butcher" was a small, gentle, pleasant looking man with blue eyes and "a lightish colored beard" (39). He was a butcher who "loved to sit and think and he loved to be important in religion." He also loved "his eating and a quiet life, he loved his Martha and his children, and mostly he liked all the world" (39). While he enjoyed his comfortable life in the old country, he could see the benefits of moving to America. His neighbors who had moved there had become very rich, and he supposed it would be best for them to get rich, too. Eventually Martha persuades him to emigrate; it was what she wanted.

What follows, then, is a brief story of what leaving one country for another feels like (*Editorial Note: one of my favorite parts of the book—CKF*). David is all in favor of Martha's plan, approving as she sells their business and most of their possessions. But when people come to pick up what they had purchased, and especially when David goes to the butcher shop that had been his, he feels overwhelmingly sad, as if "there was no place anymore anywhere for Hersland" (41). As Martha urges him onward, "he wanted to settle down again and keep staying," but he follows her, loads their wagon, and sets out for the city where a ship would take them to America. When the townspeople come to see them off, David feels good again, "important as if it were in religion," because everyone was excited for him; meanwhile, "the mother was like a great mountain, good and firm and directing" (42).

They have not gone very far before they realize that "the father was not there any longer with them" (42). Martha finds him—**"He was sitting at the first turning, looking at the village below him, at all the things he was leaving, and he simply could not endure it to him."** Martha convinces him, and (42)
he convinces himself, that he has to do what is best for his family, for his children. But as they trudge on, very tired and hot, he disappears again. Martha tells the children to keep going slowly while she goes back to find him. And find him she does, "before she had gotten back to . . . where he could see all he was going to leave behind him. She had walked faster

than he and had caught him" (44). Again, the text offers us a surprisingly
gentle family dynamic in the midst of conflict. Though Martha is clearly
in charge and fiercely determined, she is neither angry nor impatient with
David's reluctance. "**It was only a way he always had had whenever he had to**
(44) **do a new thing.**" She understands, and she walks with him talking about
how wonderful their new life will be "when they all would all get rich."
As they walk on toward the wagon, with her "telling about how good he
was to do what was best for her and the children," he begins to look sick
from heat and effort. She coaxes him into the wagon with their children,
and off they go, until they have gone too far for him to walk back.

When they make it to America, to Bridgepoint, it is hard at first, but it works out. "The sons made money for them, the daughters worked and then got married to men whom they found making money around them" (44). American dream achieved. There's a strange reference (the second) to one of their children who dies a glutton, this time noting that "spoiling him was the one weak thing the strong mother did to harm any of them" (45). Old David never makes a lot of money, but his children give him a comfortable life. When he dies he leaves his wife a nice sum of money. She, of course, "lived long and was strong to the last and firmly supporting and her back was straight and firm and always she was like a great mountain" (45). After suffering two strokes, she dies, and so does her generation.

And we're on to the next generation, and to David and Martha's
children, "almost all of [whom] were prosperous" (45). The gluttonous
one is referenced again; he dies and leaves a wife and children unprovided
for, so his brothers support them. Two daughters marry well, but the
third sister marries a poorer man, so her brothers "kept her dressed and
gave her children education and then later in their life started them out
in their working" (45). The narrator interjects to point out that, "**On the
whole, it was a substantial progress the family had made in wealth, in opportunity,
in education, in following out the mother's leading to come to the new world to find**
(45) **for themselves each one a sufficient fortune.**" This sense of "progress" that the
narrator calls our attention to is equated with fortune, American-style,
but it is also connected with generosity and family support, as it's often
practiced by first-generation immigrants.

There follows a brief discussion of hereditary traits, and how Martha and David's children are a mixture of the two of them, both their flaws and strengths. The one who concerns us most, David Hersland II, is "a very splendid kind of person" (45). **"He was big and abundant and full of new ways of thinking, and this was all his mother in him, but he had not her patient
steadfast working."** He is like his father when it comes to feeling important. (45-
"But," the narrator notes, "all this will show more and more in him as I 46)
tell you slowly the history of him" (46). This is our man in Gossols—the newest part of the new world—the young man who went West "to find for himself his life and a sufficient fortune" (46). Even as a young man in Bridgepoint he was rich enough to support a wife and children, he was already eager to head West. The story continues with David's marriage to "little Fanny Hissen," arranged by his sister Martha in an effort to keep him near her.

As the narrator returns to tracing inherited qualities, we find out that Fanny's mother is the one we call "Good Grandmother #3," the "gentle little hopeless one who wept out all the sorrow for her children" (47). Fanny, too, is sweet and gentle, one of "many and such pleasant little children" of "a hard father and a dreary mother" (47). The narrator takes a minute to remark on the mother's "sad trickling"; even joy and laughter for her had sadness behind it. And the narrator is fine with that. They quote (without quotation marks) Proverbs 14:13: "for even in laughter the heart is sorrowful and the end of that mirth is heaviness," then credits "the quaker woman" for that insight. Then they conclude: **"I often think if I could be so fixed as never to laugh or smile I should be one step better, it fills
me with sorrow when I see people so full of laugh."** Is this merely wordplay, (47)
reversing sorrow and laughter to humorously highlight the contrast, or is this a truth offered up by the narrator (the creation of an author famous for her hearty laugh)?

The contrast continues with the observation that the Hissen children are a cheerful bunch, maybe because "the mother had wept out all the sorrow for them" (47). None of them are particularly ambitious but they all "lived and died in mildness and contentment." One of these small pleasant children was Fanny, now married to David Hersland II, and the two of them, hereditarily speaking, "had mixed up very well" (48). Their children, notes the narrator, are our generation, so the three who survive into adulthood will always be "young grown men and women to us."

Pages 48–55 | Those three Hersland children, Martha, Alfred, and David, become the main characters of this novel (inasmuch as there are main characters), so this is the beginning of what we will learn about them. For the next twenty pages, the text is primarily concerned with the family dynamic they grew up in, from an idyllic childhood to a more quarrelsome adolescence. They are at the center because they become so "big," in physicality as well as personality. Very soon their mother, little Fanny, "could not lead them nor could she know what they needed inside them" (48). In their eagerness to "find themselves free inside themselves," they are quickly beyond her, yet she still loves them and is proud of them. But they are self-sufficient and, because of this, come to sideline and ignore her. Their father is also proud of them, but he very much views himself as the father and head of the household, so he gets angry at his children's independence, at his lack of control over them. He tries to master them, to impose his will on them, and this becomes hard for Fanny to watch.

Thus, the three Hersland children, Alfred, Martha, and Young David, who we are about to "learn slowly the history of each," grow up strong and free inside, "big in themselves and winning" (49). Though their father encourages their independence when they are younger, "proud that they needed to win for themselves their own freedom," the three are eventually engaged in what sounds like pretty constant battle with an increasingly angry, table-pounding father (49). In this struggle, Fanny cowers on the sidelines, and is "not very important to them." This phrase is repeated frequently through these pages. It is the father who matters, the big, abundant, innovative father. We are also reminded that their home in Gossols is the perfect place to grow up:

> It was a very good kind of living the Hersland children had in their beginning, and their freedom in the ten acres where all kinds of things were growing, where they could have all anybody could want of joyous, sweating,

> of rain and wind, of hunting, of cows and dogs and horses, of chopping wood, of making hay, of dreaming, of lying in a hollow all warm with the sun shining while the wind was howling, of knowing all queer poor kinds of people that lived in this part of Gossols where the Herslands were living and where no other rich people were living. (50)

That passion for freedom, to break the bond of parental control, is stronger in the oldest child, Martha, and in the youngest child, David, who constantly searches for meaning in his life (more on that several hundred pages from now). There is a sense of freedom in Alfred (who we know is to marry Julia Dehning), but it is less pronounced.

This leads to a return to the lecture that began earlier (21) on singularity, and how sadly Alfred represents it. The return of this concept, and the reassertion of the strong first-person narrative voice, seems significant here. "Yes I say it again now to all of you," it begins (50). The truly singular must go away (presumably, again, from the U.S.). The narrator explains, "we cannot stay where there are none to know it," leaving only "a poor thing like Alfred Hersland" to represent singularity. Alfred "is a little different with it, not with real singularity to be free in it, but it is better with him than to have no one to do it," they explain. Poor representative though he is, Alfred is "all we can leave behind to show a little how some can begin to do it" (51), because, again, "vital singularity is yet an unknown product with us, we who in our habits, dress-suit cases, clothes and hats and ways of thinking, walking, making money, talking . . . all with a metallic clicking like the type-writing which is our only way of thinking." The digression concludes with a lament for the blandness of the American character: "No brother singulars, it is sad here for us, there is no place in an adolescent world for anything eccentric like us, machine making does not turn out queer things like us, they can never make a world to let us be free each one inside us." As a side (51)
note, when we all first read the novel, the phrase "brother singulars," followed by "us" here and on page 21, convinced us briefly that the narrator is gendered masculine. Other passages in the novel, however, undermine and complicate this insight, as does the co-location of the word "queer" in this passage. (See our discussion of the metafictional narrator in Chapter One).

Young David Hersland appears here, briefly, as the hope for singularity in ways his old-world father and flawed older brother can't be. Yet, we learn, he, too, falls short. He doesn't have "that vital steadfast singularity inside him that custom passion and a feel for mother earth can breed in men" (51). If you're keeping score at home, that leaves Martha as our hope for a truly singular character. But we're not there yet, as we hasten slowly forward.

"But now to make again a beginning," the narrator inserts. As we read on, the text is replete with these narrative digressions followed by an announced return to the story at hand. Beginnings abound. And this one takes us back to the family dynamic of the Herslands in Gossols, where the father "believed in hardening his children" (51). It turns out Daddy David is embarrassing his adolescent children because of the "queer ways in him." The text sets out to sketch his character; he is a great thinker and takes pride in educating his children; he starts projects easily but they do not always pan out, so he is sometimes unreliable; he is big, "big in the size of him and in his ways of thinking" (52).

And while their home is full of angry discussion "much fierce talking and much frowning," his table-pounding and patriarchal dominance, all that his "three big resentful children" have to do is remind him that they have a right to their opinions. "**You started us out in this way of doing, you**
(52-53) **have no right to change now and say that it's no way for us to be acting.**" Their father consistently believes in their individuality and their freedom.

David II also has "queer ways" of eating, and he imposes his strange habits on his children. He is, again, large, and all his life liked only large things, the one exception being his tiny wife. The narrator adds detail on detail in a series of examples of his strange behaviors. He often flip-flops, being generous one day and stingy the next. He loves to talk, and people gather to listen to him, but he never listens to his children. When he walks, his hat always looks like it will fall off, and he always seems to forget that two or three of his children are behind him. He moves his body as if he is throwing it from side to side, and he always feels important. Without paying, he grabs fruit or cakes from shops, embarrassing the children but pleasing the vendors, who know him and know he will always pay up.

He forces his children to live like they are poor as part of their "hardening" education, but they also have everything he could offer them if he imagines it would do them any good. In short, his "big freedom and this big important feeling and the big way of beginning" made "a queer man of him, an eccentric from the others around him, and all that stopped it from making a god of him was his way of being impatient inside him and not being very good at keeping going but always making for himself a new beginning" (55).

These examples continue, while the narrator reminds us intermittently of the long arc of the family storyline—that "mostly they lived very well together" on those grand ten acres; it was only later "when the father would get his very angry feeling and the mother was a little ailing and the fierce little temper broke into weakness and helplessness inside her and the three big struggling young grown men and women were seeking each one his own freedom and his own beginnings" that things got tough (54). This might be a good place to remind ourselves that this section, despite its rambling pace and constant digressions, is labeled "The Hersland Parents." Many of these stories, examples, descriptions and confrontations will reappear in the pages to come, but here we are laying our narrative foundation on the head of the Hersland family.

Pages 55–70 | We get more development of Fanny's character through these next pages, along with the requisite tracing of her genetic influences. Of the whole California Hersland family, she is the one whom the text connects most with "middle class living" and "the right way of being," but she represents it well, "keeping a good table for her husband" and "dressing herself and her children in simple expensive clothing" (56-57).[1] There are

1. In early drafts of the novel, this "right middle-class american living" was described as "german-american." It wasn't until the undated typescripts that an editor removed (in pencil) all references to "german," and so we suspect that the typescripts, or at least the careful editing of the typescripts, come well after the 1906-08 drafts, somewhere closer to WWI or perhaps in preparation for the serialization of the novel that began shortly after the end of the war.

lovely references to how affectionate she is with the children when they are little, when "they liked to cuddle to her," and, bashful in the presence of strangers, they "clung to her." The narrative sums her up repeatedly as "unimportant" and "sweet," with "a fierce little temper" which she sometimes uses to control her big husband. Other phrases, like "simple expensive clothing" and "important feeling" also appear frequently where repetition settles in to define the style of the novel, as we note in our introductory chapter on "The Modernist Sentence." In sum, though largely ignored as her children get older, Fanny is "a sweet contented little woman who lived in her husband and children" (57).

It turns out that what makes Fanny feel important is having others dependent on her, so when the children stop being dependent, she begins more forcefully asserting her influence over her staff, the "servants and governesses and seamstresses who worked for her" (57). Being well-to-do has that advantage. The status alone doesn't give her "that strong feeling of being important inside her." Exercising her privilege over others does. So, there's that. And more of it to come.

But there is also the suggestion of something more, something that comes to Fanny from Sophie Shilling. Meeting her, her sister Pauline, and their mother, Fanny "had her first important feeling" early in her time in Gossols. Is it just because she is so clearly dominant in their company? Apart from the privilege, the "dignity and beauty of right living," that she is used to, separated as she is from the sense of belonging she found at home in Bridgepoint, without ambition, excitement, or much emotion that she had enjoyed as a Hissen daughter, she has never experienced an important feeling "arise of itself from within" her, not without "the fat daughter" Sophie Shilling, "a new kind of friend to her" (61). But we'll have to wait to figure out what exactly Sophie did for her, because now, for ten pages, the narrative reviews the Hissens—the religious father, the dreary mother, and each of the right-living children—and asserts that none of them had that "important feeling" about them. "Mostly they lived and died in mildness and contentment." Not so with Fanny. "It was only way off there in Gossols, shut off from a lively feeling of living of well to do living, shut off from her friends and family feeling, that Fanny Hissen, Mrs. Hersland, could find in herself a really important feeling." (63)

And here we delve a bit more into Fanny's background. One engaging moment finds young Fanny asking her father for permission to leave for Gossols with David Hersland. This faithful father answers with a joke about a priest who, when asked by a member of his congregation whether it would be right to get a shave at a barber shop before church on Sunday, told the man "it would be a sin." Two Sundays later the man finds the freshly-shaved priest leaving the barber shop. Wait, he said, you told me I shouldn't do this, then you did it! Right, the priest said. But "I did not do any asking" (67).

One other notable passage gently describes Fanny's father's commitment to his religion as he is dying:

> He was himself all there was of him, all there was of religion, and religion was all there was of living for him, and so the dying from old age that came slowly to him all came together to be him. He was religion, death could not rob him, he could lose nothing in his dying, he was all that there was of him, all there was of religion, and religion was all there was of living, and so he, dying of old age, without struggling, met himself by himself in his dying, for religion was everlasting, and so for him there could be no ending, he and religion and living and dying were all one and everything and every one and it was for himself that he was one, living, dying, being, and religion. (68)

Here we find the narrative addressing similar concerns as many American women's novels of the time addressed, but without dismissing or rejecting them, as modernist writers would come to do. The generosity here is striking, as old man Hissen is allowed his nineteenth-century beliefs without a whiff of condescension or existential angst from the narrator. And then the story moves on to note again that the father and the mother were "mixed up" in all the Hissen children, including Fanny, even years later after living far away from them. They all had "dreary trickling" or "that stubborn feeling" or "sweetness in them" or angry feelings "that came in flashes" (68–72).

And we encounter another beginning, back to when David Hersland married Fanny Hissen, and then to "Martha, Alfred, and young David, and these three are of them who are to be always in this history of us young grown men and women to us" (72). But we can't move forward in our family saga without remembering "the knowledge of the men and women who as parents and grandparents came together and mixed up to make us and we must have always in us a lively sense of these mothers and these fathers, of how they lived and married and then they had us and we came to be inside us in us" (72). An individual is made in a context, and understanding the context, how it "slowly came to make us," is to know ourselves. So, on we go, slowly.

Pages 73–83 | But first, another detour. The narrator has Things To Say about American marriage. The two-page (sometimes sexist, generally heteronormative) riff on what it takes to get men and women into marriage begins by asserting that: "**In American teaching marrying is just loving but that is not enough**
(73) **for marrying.**" Even when there are many available "decent well to do men," marriage requires a push from a mother or a sister, particularly when men get older and are less "lively in the feeling of loving." When the potential groom gets "fixed in his ways of living" (like Alfred Hersland), he needs a married sister who feels "strongly inside [her] the need that all the world keep on going" to urge him forward (74). "Loving is good," the narrator informs us, "but it needs coaxing, arranging, flattering, teasing, urging, a little good tempered irritated forcing, or else the man will forget all about his loving" (74-75). This passage challenges the tradition of the romantic novel, with a single young woman at the center and love in the air. This novel won't be adding to that mythology, we are informed. That American teaching about loving "is all mostly lying" (74). Here, we're going to see how that conjugal sausage gets made. "It is the truth that I have been telling," the narrator concludes (75). And we continue by going back to the marriage of Fanny Hissen and David Hersland, overtly arranged by David's sister Martha.

But first our own detour. In this novel ostensibly about middle class living, the narrator points out twice in this brief reflection on marriage that "The American teaching [about loving and marrying] is very well for young people or for poor ones or for those who are strong in a sense of loving, who have a lively sense of wanting, who have strongly the instinct for mating, but for most of them, the well to do, comfortable men and women, it takes more to make a marriage for them" (74). This novel is a specific, albeit fictional, case study of a privileged American family and their "right way of living," and with that we often get dismissive or insulting comments about the poor or lower class. Are passages like these an ironic send-up of middle-class American values, or are they an unvarnished assertion of them?

As we find out more about the elder Martha and her thoughtful selection of Fanny to be her brother's wife, Stein's experimental style takes over for several pages. A few insights about Martha are repeated and rearranged in what stands out as the first of many efforts to understand character through reiteration, from different angles, in various combinations. We see Martha by way of her brother, the Hissen women and their father, and Martha's husband. Here Martha is "not a strong woman," but she is "a strong enough woman" (77, 79). She is "not very pleasing, in some ways she was very pleasing" (77). She has "an important feeling," but not in religion, and she pursues "the right way to do in the business of living" (79). While the Hissen women find her "common," she is "not low in feeling" (79). In fact, her "hard feeling" yields "right judging" (80). Wrapping it up, we find that to Martha's sentimental husband, who "had much very soggy passion in him," Martha was "altogether pleasing" (82. To the Hissen men and women, "Martha was a good woman," but "not really pleasing" (83). And, most importantly for this moment: **"To her brother she was not really pleasing but she was a good enough woman for him to choose a wife for him to content him."** (83)

Pages 84–92 | We return, then, to Fanny (now Hersland) and the beginnings of her self-importance while living near the Shillings in a hotel in California. Within the Hissen family, she could never get a sense of her individuality, but contrasting now with "old heavy flabby Mrs. Shilling and her fat daughter Sophie and the other daughter the thinner Pauline Shilling," Fanny apparently begins to see that she is no ordinary woman

(84). The Shillings take some real hits here as the text homes in on their "queerness." Was something "left out of them" or did it come from "something queer inside in all them" (84-85)? Before some hilarious descriptions of their "big doughy empty heads," they are summed up as "just ordinary stupid enough women like millions of them" (85). The go-to words in these paragraphs are, suggestively, "fat" and "queer." Though the two daughters are sisterly with one another, their relationship is dominated not by age but size: "it is the fat one who is afraid of the other because it would hurt more if pins were stuck into her . . . there is so much more unprotected surface to her" (86). And that's how it was with Sophie.

Fanny's relationship to Sophie seems to be the most significant of the three, but the details are (as usual) contradictory and difficult to sort out. "Sophie Shilling never meant very much to her" is followed by "Always she had a feeling for Sophie Shilling" (87). We find that Pauline is more distinctive. "There have been always many millions made just like the mother and the fatter sister Sophie Shilling but there have never been so many millions made altogether like the thinner sister Pauline Shilling" (88). Contrasting the sisters, these next paragraphs circle around the poles of queerness, size, fear, and, finally, emptiness. One paragraph describing the thinner Pauline moves playfully from "hole" to "whole" as it examines her incompleteness (90).

We return to the mother's "head like a baby's, wobbly on her" (91), followed by summary of Mrs. Hersland's relationship with them: "**She always had a feeling for Sophie Shilling but she had no affection for her, Sophie was not in any way important to her, Mrs. Hersland never came to feel any nearer**
(92) **to the mother and the sister Pauline Shilling.**" While the three Shillings lived near the young Hersland couple in the hotel for a year, "after leaving the hotel [Mrs. Hersland] never saw much of them" (92).

So why are they important? Why do they dominate this section and return often in the pages that follow? Ostensibly because these relationships first gave Mrs. Hersland, little Fanny Hissen, her "possible almost important feeling" (92). And that feeling begins to grow "a little from her husband and making him do things from her compelling, but mostly from her dependents, the governesses seamstresses servants and the others, for her poor queer people who soon came to be always around her" (92).

Pages 93–104 | The story returns to David the father, then, enumerating his distinctive qualities (big, uneven, and "full up inside him") and developing, through repetition, his relationship with Fanny. To David, his wife's power "was a joke"; he sees her as a decorative, like a flower, as "just a woman to content him" (93). He, like many strong men, needs only women who are useful to him "like any other object in the world around him," a chair or a train engine (94). Fanny works for him because of her "brilliant seductive managing" that gives her "power with him," even while he can "forget that she was existing" (95). As a young, vigorous man he doesn't need her to fill him, but it would "come to be clear in his later living," when his wife was long dead, that "he needed much more than she had ever been to fill him up inside him" (97). One very long sentence (beginning near the middle of page 96 with "His wife Fanny Hersland" and extending through the bottom of that page) twists and turns and austerely sums up the emotional component of David's feeling for Fanny over the course of their lives together.

But here they are, a young couple with three children, "servants and governesses and dependents" on that ten acres in Gossols. David passes his time with rich men, "making his great fortune," and Fanny spends her days with the poorer people "and she was of them and always was above them and in the same way she was with them the poor, for her, queer people around them" (97). We're reminded that there "was much pleasure" and freedom in their living then; "It was very joyous for all of them the days of the beginning of their living" (98):

> The sun was always shining for them, for years after to all three of the children, Sunday meant sunshine and pleasant lying on the grass with a gentle wind blowing and the grass and flowers smelling, it meant good eating, and pleasant walking, it meant freedom and the joy of mere existing, it meant the pungent smell of cooking, it meant the full satisfied sense of being stuffed up with eating, it meant sunshine and joking, it meant laughing and fooling, it

> meant warm evenings and running, and in the winter that had its joys too of indoor living and outside the wind would be blowing and the owls in the
> (98) walls scaring you with their tumbling.

Leaving their haven to visit rich people is hard for the children, who "would shrink behind the mother" and experience that "half and half being" of country kids in the city (99, 100). Given the circumstances, it seems no wonder that the three of them feel "a real part of the living of the poorer people who were around them," and all three hold onto that sensibility until "later in their living" (101). This country connection is the focus of exposition over the next several pages, as we become acquainted with some of the neighbors "living in small houses around them" (104).

Pages 104–130 | Some of these poorer homes are headed by women, and "with some there was no mother" (104). Some fathers and brothers have mysterious jobs, including one who works in "an intelligence office," during the day, "but there is nothing bad about them." In short, "they were all honest enough and good enough men and women with decent enough children" and Martha, David, and Alfred live among them, never asking questions, "never asking what they did for a living" (105). The text shifts to highlight one particular family with three daughters, Anna and Cora and Bertha. While the mother is "a foreigner," a hard-working dressmaker who "never had a past, present or future connected with her," living as she does, in the moment, she is "very much existing" for all five of the Herslands. Unlike her husband, who may or may not have been a foreigner, and "was not existing for them," working during the days, then coming home only to eat and sleep (107). Working men like him need other men to make them feel important, the narrator intones. "[I]t is only when other men meet with them that the existence gets to be strong enough in them so that any one can know them and they can feel it in them that they are men and one with all the men around them, when they are alone with women and children they have never in them
(108) anything of such a feeling."

Anna and Cora and Bertha go "through the changes" one at a time, and their mother observes "each one [who] had been inside her" (110).

She is "old now and little wooden," but her oldest daughter, Anna is in her prime and "had come to be a rather beautiful woman." In fact, "this change into beauty" happens to each of them. The narrative reexamines the ideas of "existence" and "importance" then, telling us that Anna has importance inside her, like her father, but not so much existence as her mother; she has enough existence, though, to underline her importance so that everyone around her can feel it, including, we assume, those Hersland kids. Cora has less importance and less existence in her; Bertha has the least, less than "any of them except the father" (114). No one considers him, though. "This family to every one who knew them was a family of women" (117).

The next in the neighborhood to draw our attention is the Richardson family, Mr. Richardson, "a tall thin blond man" (repeatedly) and his two children, Eddy and Lilly—"there was no wife to him or mother to the children then" (119). They are notable because, like many around them in Gossols, they are a religious family. For them, "religion would always be in them like eating and sleeping and washing, not like breathing and loving" (119). Religion makes Mr. Richardson "important to everyone who knew him" (110).

Our narrator, who apparently can't pass up an opportunity to talk about washing, then expounds on religion's connection to daily ritual. **"Eating and sleeping are not like loving and breathing. Washing is not like eating and sleeping. Believing is like breathing and loving. Religion can be believing, it can be like breathing, it can be like loving, it can be like eating and sleeping, it can be like washing."** Mr. Richardson had always had religion in him; it "was (121)
always natural in him" (121).

The Hersland children encounter their poorer neighbors in "in their daily living" and come to be "more entirely of them" than they were of their mother" (123). The story winds back to remind us that this is "a detailed history of each one of the three of them," so we will find out more about these neighbors as we study each Hersland. These reminders help ground our reading of this novel that (now, and even more so later) seems to be spinning out from its center, off track and away from the focus it claims in the lives of the three Herslands. We often find lead-ins to these reorientations—"As I was saying" and "To begin again, then" (123). So here, beginning again, we return to the Hersland children's relationship to their mother, who became less and less important to them until "she died away from all of them" (124).

Then, for the next three pages, the text zooms out again, away from the Herslands, to observe "many kinds of men, of every kind of them there are many millions of them many millions always made to be like the others of that kind of them, of some kinds of them there are more millions made like the others of such a kind of them than there are millions made alike of some other kinds of men" (126). Repeated consideration of importance, individual being, age and size, strength and patience are surrounded by constant references to "millions" and "kinds of," until we return to the orbit of the Hersland family with an "As I have been saying" (128). In this way the novel delivers a sense of the father's particularity and his commonality, his unique relation to his specific family, and how ordinary it was for him to be distanced from them.

David's ways of educating his children, of doctoring them, of guiding their eating, and of dominating them with outbursts and "impatient feeling" are at play in these pages. We learn that "**His children had it in them, in the way that almost all children have it in them, his children had it in them for a**
(129) **long time to be afraid of him.**" But less than most children of most fathers, and less and less as they grow older and recognize that "there was not any more, for them, anything to fear from him" (129). "As I was saying" appears in nearly every paragraph for a few pages as the narrator reviews what we know about the Herslands and prompts us toward their future to come in the pages ahead of us. Martha, for example, had it in her to be like her father, "but all this will come out later in the history of her as she grew older as she went away from all of them and then came back out of her trouble" (134).

David's assessments of his family and theirs of him are reasserted here, with comparisons based on "bigness," "impatient feeling," and "importance." The eldest, Alfred, "had it in him to see the bigness in his father" (134), while there was always with David, the youngest, "a little in him of contempt" for his father's inconsistency. His father's tendency to be always beginning, then to "be full up with impatient feeling and then he would be changing and then he would push everything away from him" irritates the younger David. We get some additional details about the ten acres—"dogs and chickens and sometimes ducks and turkeys in the yard then, they had horses and two cows"—where their way of life "was regular enough," and "their living was pleasant and interesting" (136–7). The narrative here treats the Herslands as one unit in one paragraph, then distinguishes them in the next, sometimes individually, sometimes dividing children and parents. We learn that each of the children "were different each one of them from the others of them in the troubles they had inside them, in the lonely feeling they had sometimes in them that each one was alone inside" (138).

The idea of "repeating what is inside them so that any one can know them" begins here and will come to control the text. It is, again, Stein's method of character development, of understanding the "fundamental nature" of each of them (139). This sentence becomes typical of the style and themes of this section: "As I was saying they were regular enough in their daily living, regular as living comes to be in later living, regular in repeating but, as I was saying, in the regular repeating in mostly all children there is less that is really
from them more that is just part of the regular living around them." The narrator (139)
also begins to frame the idea of slowly revealing the novel's somewhat central plot of the development of each of the three Hersland children through constant repetition, but they do so as if the novel were constantly in flux, always under construction. "I am thinking with each one of the three of them soon now there must be a beginning," they divulge, ". . . so slowly we can know it about them" (140).

But then they return our focus to that big, domineering father, adding details to underline his eccentricities. It seems he would get his kids to start playing cards with his him, then abruptly decide that "I haven't time to go on playing" (141). He would turn his cards over to the governess, and leave all of them stuck playing a game they never would have started in the first place. "It was a small thing but it happened very often to them and it was annoying for them" (141). Next, we reexamine the mother's lack of importance to her children and husband, and swing in for one more look at that "real country living" that all three Hersland children enjoyed

(142). Finally, we compare the three—the father, with "city being," the mother and her "rich city country house living," and those three "real country living" kids who had "a mixed thing in them of the three ways of feeling, rich city country house being and city being, and the mixtures of these three feelings in each of the three of them to the people in the small houses near them" (144). This mixed experience affected all three differently, with only the youngest, David, making real country living a part of "his later living."

The next shiny distraction to divert our narrator's attention is the governess Madeleine Wyman, who tends to Fanny when she is dying and never forgets her. She is married then, "but always Mrs. Hersland was the most important thing, to her, that had even been in her" (147). She'll return at the end of this section, then again later in the text, but for now we are simply introduced to her and given a heads-up about "struggles with the family of the Wymans who wanted to interfere with her" (147). The narrator refocuses on the children and their fear of their father; they return to "millions of men," and begin to speculate about what makes one man, like David, unique among those millions.

Most significantly, the text introduced the idea of "bottom nature" here, a concept that will soon become quite (really *quite*) familiar. "The bottom to every one then is the kind of being in them that makes them," the narrator observes (149). To prepare for what follows, let's take a moment here to examine carefully the idea of "bottom nature." The narrator will later redefine and characterize many "kinds of natures," as they "are in almost all men and almost all women" (149). But for now, we should think about "the bottom" as "what makes him, it makes for him the kind of thinking, the way of eating, the way of drinking, the way of loving, the way of beginning, and the way of ending, in him" (149). So, when we delve into the extensive typology, the classification of every kind of nature (and, we assure you, we will), we should remember that everyone has a mixture of other kinds of natures with their bottom nature. And "this mixture in them with the amount they have in them of their bottom kind of nature in them makes in each one a different being from the many millions always being made like him" (149). We then begin the cataloging, but mainly with

reference to David and Fanny. The narrator points out that it is easier to know the bottom nature of people as they grow older, because it is revealed most apparently in the repetitions that make up their lives. **"Slowly, more and more, one gets to know them a repeating comes out in them."** And that, (151)
simply, is how this novel aims to develop and understand its characters.

For the final ten pages of this section, then, we roll that idea around, revisiting David's nature over the course of his life, especially through "his middle living" in Gossols, the part that most concerns the Hersland children. As we go along "there is more simple repeating" of the idea of repeating (154), of Mr. Hersland's impatience, his habit of always beginning, his "bigness," his success and wealth, and the way had of "brushing people away from before him" (155). Qualities are added here—that he "was strong in fighting," that he was susceptible to "ingratiating diplomatic domineering," and that "in his business living . . . some were afraid of him" (158). Because they lived with him and witnessed the repetitions of his behaviors, David's wife and children knew his nature better than those who encountered him in the business world. Fanny knew first "how far the nature in him would carry him" because she had "this in her from living with him as a wife to him, from the simple repeating that a man has in him for the woman who is a wife to him" (161).

This section ends and the next begins with the phrase "A man in his living has many things inside him" (163, 164). The natures of the millions and our narrator's attention to the particularity of David inform where we are and where we are going as we hasten slowly forward to the section that promises to focus on Fanny and her children.

[MRS. HERSLAND AND THE HERSLAND CHILDREN]

Pages 164–174 | Despite the section break (added from Stein's 1935 abridged version, bracketed, with a new subtitle that did not appear in the original 1925 definitive edition), we continue, almost word for word, where we left off in the previous section, philosophically, with how a man's "bottom nature" affects the way he chooses to live his life. The tone

is melodic, as Stein repeats some words and not others, rearranging, regrouping. The narrator characteristically refocuses us on David with "As I was saying," then proceeds to point out "**At the beginning of the ending of the middle living of vigorous active men and women, ways of thinking, ways of working, ways of beginning, ways of ending, ways of believing come to be in them as simple**
(166) **repeating.**" Men and women share overlapping qualities, the narrator notes, but careful readers, attentive to repetition, will observe that the repeated qualities line up in a way unique to each individual.

And here we get the professorial narrator voice, observing and classifying, interpreting and remarking. A man's feelings of self-importance are tied to bottom nature, they remind us; however, these feelings also stem from how important he is perceived to be by others. As Stephen Meyer explains in his Introduction to the 1995 Dalkey edition, and the 2025 Essentials edition of *TMOA*, "It is how one feels one's difference—one's specific form of self-importance—which determines what kind of person one is" (xxiii). The narrator asserts that each type of nature within a person is different, and the degree to which that nature affects them also varies. For example, many men are quite sure they are the most important asset to the world, whereas others see that assurance for what it is: ridiculous. The former would have a much smaller degree of "self-importance" inside of them than the latter, because theirs is tied more to how the world perceives them. To sum up: "**As I was saying men have in them their individual feeling in their way of feeling it in them about themselves to themselves inside them about**
(167-168) **the ways of being they have in them.**"

Further, our core traits influence the way we interact with the world—our many ways of living, eating, drinking, sleeping, and loving. The narrator then homes in on loving, as we review again the relationship between David and Fanny. At first, he had a tender feeling for her, but then she became less important, until, finally, she "came to be a joke to him, later then she came to be brushed away from him" (169). On the next page, "he mostly then forgot about her and that was the end of her living" is added to this repeated sequence (170). Through these iterations, the picture begins to round out more, to a deeper perception of David's dismissiveness and Fanny's loss. As the narrator catalogues the many millions of kinds of men and their various ways of loving, we learn that David "was not very strong in loving" (173).

We also learn that men like David need women later in their lives to maintain the "warm feelings" inside of them. There came a time when he needed "another kind of woman" from Fanny, who, again, drew out his tenderness early on. He needed "not a beautiful thing inside him to be in him as a tender feeling but a thing to be alive, domineering, diplomatic, moving, entering under his skin by feeling herself him managing him and important to him in her filling him where he was shrunk away from the outside of him" (174). The suggestion is that he later sees women on the side. The narrator is discreetly (and blessedly) vague on the details of this arrangement.

Pages 175–210 | We finally come, ten pages into "Mrs. Hersland and the Hersland Children," to focus on Fanny, the titular star of this section, her "important feeling," and her loneliness. This time we get more information about her character and her circumstances, as the narrator explains in a brutally honest tone that she is a small, weak woman. Leading up to her death, Fanny's life has become distant from David's; she spends more time with the servants and with her poor neighbors than with her own now-wealthy family. But being with the servants and growing increasingly distant from the habits of her privileged childhood seem to make her happier and allow her to feel important. The narrator claims that there are many ways people can gain feelings of self-importance—through religion, clothing choice, ways of loving others, and expression of anger. Because Fanny's self-esteem depends mainly on what her husband thinks of her, she feels most important while her husband still *believes* she's important. We flag these passages as one of the places in the novel where the narrator most clearly asserts middle-class values around gender.

The text brings up women's loneliness as separate from men's by asserting that women can never truly feel as lonely as men feel because "some one will take care of them, something will save them" (176). Their world can never come crashing completely down around them because they will be saved from danger by somebody else (the implication is that the "somebody else" will be gendered male). Mrs. Hersland, for her part, falls back on her Hissen upbringing, the ways of her wealthy family, for comfort. Like her "dreary trickling" mother, though, she still doesn't feel important despite her heaping piles of privilege (177). The narrator asserts that many women do not believe that bad things will happen to them because they are very trusting, as with Julia Hersland's (false) positive impressions of Alfred before their marriage draws near. The narration seems to accuse women of waiting for someone to solve their problems for them and refers to this concept a few pages later as "aggressive optimism" (184).

This is where the narrator begins the task of cataloging types of women the way they have been categorizing men; this systematic classification predominates for several pages (and, to be honest, it continues throughout the rest of the novel): "**There are then two kinds of women, those who have dependent independence in them, those who have in them independent dependence**
(186) **inside them.**" The first kind "always somehow own the ones they need to love them"; Mrs. Hersland is this kind. The return of both the Shillings and Madeleine Wyman, the women Fanny had power over, underlines this point. In the pages that follow we meet or revisit several of the "governesses, seamstresses and servants," including "foreign women," that came through that country house in Gossols. The narrator warns us that "There are many kinds of women then and many kinds of men and this then will be a history of some of the many kinds of them" (182). And a few pages later they reengage us with the task at hand—that this "will be a history of each one who ever was or is or can be living" (201):

> **When you come to feel the whole of anyone from the beginning to the ending, all the kind of repeating there is in them, all the kinds of things and mixtures in each one, anyone can see then by looking hard at any one living near them that a history of every one must be a long one. A history of any one must be a long one, slowly it comes out from them from their beginning to their ending, slowly you can see it in them the nature and the mixtures in them, slowly everything comes out from each one in the kind of repeating each one does in the different parts and kinds of living they have in them, slowly then the history of each of them comes out from them, slowly then any one**
> (201–202) **who looks well at any one will have the history of the whole of that one.**

This pep talk seems appropriately placed, as the task of describing all human types begins to completely overwhelm the traditional novel-like plot. And the repetition that has been somewhat charming up to this point begins to get tedious. It's comforting to know that Stein knows, or that she allows her narrator to acknowledge, the challenges. Here, the challenge is that this truly is going to be "a long one," that we've only just begun to read, and that what's ahead will, the narrator promises, move *slowly*.

Back to those Hersland children, the story we are ambling toward. If we want to understand the three of them, we apparently need to understand Fanny. And to understand Fanny, we will look at her in context. Who was around her in Gossols? Who did she spend time with? What made her feel important? What behaviors does she repeat? How does this reveal her character? As we slowly, continually address these questions, the narrator leads us down side-paths and across concepts—loving, resisting, attacking, weakness, bottom nature, and "servant girl being" (189). Through their childhood and young adulthood in Gossols, the Hersland children have three governesses. The narrator points out that one was foreign and two were American, highlighting, again, the idea of immigration and what it takes to become "American." Later they reference "young foreign girls or foreign American ones" (188). While most of the servants in their home were German, "sometimes they could not get them" so they ended up with "an Irishwoman, twice Italian women, once a Mexican" (187). The children tease these women because they have "queerness" in them "from cooking, from cleaning and from lonesome living, from their sitting in the kitchen, from having a mistress to direct them" (187). Not the Germans, though. They were "steady women, they did not have anything of such a queerness in them" (187).

For a paragraph, the narrator focuses on one particular servant who, like most of them, stays a long time, "a blond little woman" who can't cook or clean. She lies. "She had little curls in her blond hair" and "the little dirty shrinking lying blond hair nature in her" (189). So, she didn't work out. We suspect Mr. Hersland's unmet needs may have had something to do with this.

The narrator takes this as a jumping off place for further repetition, as

that "little girl sweet shrinking little lying nature" and a "grimy little girl nature" characterize some servant girls, and as the cataloging of the "many millions" of women continues. "As I was saying" interrupts this litany for a moment to bring us back to Mrs. Hersland and her preference for older servants (with a suggestion, again, that Mr. Hersland was not to be trusted). A few pages of rumination on servant girl types and another "As I was saying," and we are back with Mrs. Hersland in Gossols, summing up what we know about the servants who lived with her over the years and remembering that this novel sometimes aspires to be **"a history of every one**
(194) **who ever can or is or was or will be living"** Between the lines of the narrative of the Hersland family, the confident narrator presses on in the task of creating a history of all types of people. This passionate desire to categorize is reflected in how they point out that not only "bottom natures," but also the mixtures of qualities in each person are important because so many qualities are jumbled within people in so many different combinations that millions of people end up having the same qualities—but in different amounts. "As one sees every on in their living, in their loving, sitting, eating, drinking, sleeping, walking, working, thinking, laughing, as any one sees all of them from their beginning to their ending" we can get a better sense of the history of each of them—and, thus, of all of them (197).

The different types of people we meet here are often reintroduced using variations of previous sentences. These repeated sentences sometimes have different verb tenses, where one sentence can pertain to a different time period than the sentence before it, so readers have to stay on their toes to figure out which part of the Herslands' lives they are observing. The narrator cues this fact with the note, "I said each repeating in each one has each time in it a little changing" (211). They insist that the whole being inside everyone comes across in their repeating, over time, actions, decisions, thoughts, and beliefs, which all make up their bottom natures.

Mrs. Hersland has decided preferences about which types of servants she wants around; most particularly, "she likes to be of them and above them" (206). The narrator suggests that because Fanny believes in her own superiority, in her own "virtue or goodness" she becomes "injured and angry" when she perceives that her servants wrong her (208). That little blond woman clearly got on her last nerve and gave her "a bright angry feeling" (207). And lest we forget, "Mrs. Hersland had in her living, mostly in the beginning and in the middle of her middle living very much of such feeling" (207). It was her "resisting way of being" and her "dependent independence" that sometimes looked like attacking and that sometimes had "stubbornness or weakness in it" (209).

Following this information about Fanny, the narrator intrudes again, discussing how individual repeating turns into a revelation of types and ultimately creates history—our repeating makes us who we are; it's something we all share. "Repeating then is always coming out of every one, always in the repeating of every one and coming out of them there is a little changing" (210). These subtle changes are what give us individuality, and this repetitious character development is the secret to understanding this truth: "**The history of each one then is a history of that one and a piece of the history of their kind of men and women.**" (210) Through reproducing another's acts and language we get access to distinct characters—and a better understanding of all characters, of their history and culture. Here the text seems to be angling to become what we will later call, via Roland Barthes, "a tissue of quotations," drawn from "innumerable centers of culture," revealing something different with each interaction.

Pages 211-231 | While persistently claiming this larger project of understanding everyone (*Editorial Note: I can't help but think of Casaubon's ill-fated "Key to All Mythologies" in* Middlemarch—*CKF*), the novel draws us back into Mrs. Hersland's life ("As I was saying"), homing in on one particular dress maker, Lillian Rosenhagen, a prototype of "anxious feeling" (213). "Anxious feeling was in her always inside her coming to be strong in her whenever any little new thing was demanded of her." The narrator clearly feels sorry for anxious people, finding it unfortunate that they must live a life full of anxiety, but nonetheless concluding that all people have some "anxious being" inside of them. Large, tall, and black-haired, Lillian was "a stupid woman and never said anything but [for some reason] the children could never forget having had her in the house with them" (214). Oh, and she also "had a very unpleasant nature" (214). The characterization of Lillian requires repeating the messages of anxiety, stupidity, disagreeableness and spinsterhood in various formations for several pages.

Like the Shilling family, the Rosenhagens, too, have a mother and two sisters (the father "is not living"). Lillian is the older sister by four years; "the mother was old then and did nothing but a little cleaning and cooking;" and the younger sister, Cecilia, seems to be equally unpleasant and anxious as Lillian, but without her sewing skills. Each sister has her own "stupid being" inside of her because, of course, types of stupid being vary. The narrator then goes on to distinguish the two sisters through their repetitions and by way of their bottom natures. Lillian gets characterized as having, "as a bottom her indolent and stupid being," while Cecilia has "anxious feeling as the bottom and whole of her being" (218).

The comparison of the two sisters continues, off and on, for several pages. We learn that, while both were spinsters, "Cecilia Rosenhagen was a true spinster" by nature, not, like her sister, who by circumstance—"no man came to ever want to marry her" (220). In these pages, tiny shifts like this one, describing why they weren't married, become significant: **"In Lillian's case it was that no man had ever come to want her, no man ever wanted to have**
(220) **Cecilia; that was quite a different matter"**. We meet a few other dressmakers, "three sets of women" who made clothes for Fanny and young Martha, and insights about their natures blends with our study of the Rosenhagens. And then we meet Mary Maxworthing, the dressmaker who made Fanny's fancy dresses.

Lucky for Mary, she has "independent dependent being" with "attacking in her" but not much fighting, "almost nothing of anxious being," little "impatient being," and no "stupid bottom to her" (225). In fact, "she had very little stupid being in her," *and* she was a good dressmaker (not as good as her "business partner" Mabel, though). The narrator promises that we will understand better the differences between Mary and the many millions of others "later in the history of the Hersland daughter Martha, in the history of Julia Dehning" (225). So that's still ahead, another promise for those who stick with it and keep reading. The narrator compares Mary with the other single women, Lillian and Cecilia, by way of their natures and beings, and points out that Mary "had men who wanted her to marry them, and when she was thirty-five she did marry and she married very well then, not well enough to give up dress-making but well enough to be very comfortable in living" (226). Mary is sensible, a generous and compassionate woman with a lot of patience. More on her in a moment.

But for now, let's pause and admire some of our favorite pages where the narrator reflects on this premise: "**Stupid being then is in every one.**" (We put this motto on our *Making of Americans* t-shirts.) "As I was saying every one has stupid being in them," the narrator points out (227). What does that mean, you ask? "Stupid being is not foolish being, it is not dull or senseless being, it is sometimes foolish being, it is sometimes dull or senseless being, it is not always any very certain kind of being, it is always in each one and sometimes it come in some fashion out of every one" (227). Apparently, stupid being is universal. "Each one as I was saying has in them their kind of stupid being, the kind of stupid being that is natural to their kind of them" (227). And here we are, about to begin "a history of stupid being in some" (206). Both of us believe that Stein is playing here, laughing affectionately at human nature and sharing a joke with her readers. Yes, we all agree, people can be ridiculously stupid. But, this novel seems to say, here are some interesting ones worth spending a few pages with.

And thank goodness we have Mary, who "really had very little stupid being in her" (228). At bottom, she was all gayety and sympathy. She escaped from the family farm to Gossols and worked for a time taking care of children," which she didn't like. With her entrepreneurial spirit, she wanted more freedom, so she sent for her relative ("the daughter of a cousin of Mary's sister-in-law"), Mabel Linker, and worked as a governess until Mabel learned "cutting and fitting and dress-making from the beginning" (228). Mary put every penny into their first dress shop, but it wasn't successful because the two women couldn't drum up enough business to stay afloat. They began to fight, though they stayed together, taking care of one another. The ambitious Mary took the business failure harder than Mabel did, and she was forced afterward to rely on Mabel, who, despite being flighty was really talented and kept working as a dressmaker. Mary goes back to nannying, and of course feels like a total failure at life, with

“a very near despairing feeling” (231). But there’s something about Mary.
(231) **“Every one who knew her had a certain feeling about her.”** She was hard-working reliable and ambitious, and she had “no wildness or recklessness in her being” (231).

Pages 232–260 | What a surprise then, when something unexpected happens to Mary. One day, she goes to the doctor. Even though she’s described as having very little “recklessness or wildness in her,” she finds out that she’s pregnant (233). The doctor she visits insists (three times) “you know what’s the matter with you,” and Mary insists in return that she does not. He thinks she’s lying to him because she feels very little shame or anxiety, just “impatient feeling in her.” Clearly, this makes the young male doctor angry (“angry” is repeated four times in two paragraphs). He tells her “You’d better get him to marry you” (234). Well, this advice goes unheeded. “She did not then say anything further, she was not interested in what the doctor had further to say to her” (234). She goes home, and the text tells us (again, three times) that “it got told to Mabel Linker,” “It was told to Mabel Linker,” and “Mary Maxworthing told it very directly to her.” Mabel was the first to know about the baby. “I don’t care,” Mary says, “I want a baby, so much the worse for me getting it in this way but I want it anyway” (234).

Of course, both women know that people will talk. “One would have thought surely Mary Maxworthing would make a man marry her before such a thing would happen to her” (234), but there is no man in this story for now—only Mary and Mabel. We get a bit more of their history, revisiting their early days together when “Mary almost idolized” Mabel, calling her “angel Mabel” (236). The narrator then opines: **“There are many ways then that people have affection in them, there are many ways of having feeling about people near one. Each one then has their own way of having affectionate feeling in them. Every one has their own kind of affectionate being. Mary Maxworthing had her way of feeling about Mabel Linker, Mabel had her own way of having**
(237) **loving feeling.”** What we will have now is “a history of the affectionate feeling and loving feeling Mary Maxworthing and Mabel Linker had in them and how each one affected the other one of them” (237). And for

the next twenty pages, weaving in and out of narrative mode, repeating, reclassifying, restating, we get their story.

The narrator points out that both of them will marry men eventually, but Mary values her freedom, her ability to control her own life, while Mabel thinks freedom comes when you love "only one man" (237). And we begin again with classification of types, as the narrative analyzes Mabel, her lack of motivation, her stupid being, and her independent dependent nature. In fact, over the next several pages the narrator keeps turning over "independent dependent being" again and again, as one of the larger overall classifications of being, characterizing both Mabel and Mary, though at different extremes. They promise we will also see independent dependent being in Martha Hersland and her father, and in Julia Dehning, among others. (*Editorial Note: if I have to read another description of independent dependents, I'm throwing the novel in the fireplace—JS.*) For future reference, the opposites, the "dependent independents" will include the other two Hersland children, Alfred and David. In this section, characters are organized by their being, sometimes in man/woman pairs, and by the smaller overlapping beings within them. Fighting, attacking, sensitive being, injured feeling, and angry feeling are just a few examples of the nuances to being that the narrator discusses, as they reassert that, "As I was saying then, every one has in them their own way of being and this comes out of them in repeating that is always in every one . . . it is all through their living always coming out of them." (248)

But back to Mabel and Mary: "As I was saying pairing of friends and pairing in loving is always a repeating of the coming together of the kinds of them" (244). While this pair, Mabel and Mary, "were not altogether successful friends," they obviously love each other. We learn that Mary's baby is stillborn at six months, and that Mabel takes care of her through that harrowing, near-death experience. "Later they had serious trouble with each other" and they didn't see much of each other for a few years (245). We review the stages of Mary and Mabel's relationship repeatedly, the ups and downs and intimacies and separations, the feelings of ingratitude and bitterness. Mary's reference to "Mabel is an angel, angel Mabel" comes up multiple times, underlining her strong feelings for Mabel, feelings

Mabel clearly doesn't reciprocate. "And then Mabel Linker had her lover, Mary found ingratitude then in her, things got so they could no longer live together" (252).

When they separate, Mary becomes spiteful and sometimes nasty to Mabel, while Mabel, as usual, is indifferent. There's a vignette where Mabel's mother-in-law works to separate the two of them, and insists that Mary not be invited to the wedding. Mary suggests that perhaps Mabel's new family should buy her a new sewing machine since they love her so much. Mabel marries, Mary inherits some money, the mother-in-law dies, and the dress-making business is re-established in "that part of Gossols where richer people were living," (enter the Herslands) and is finally successful. Then we learn that all this time Mary has been seeing the same wealthy man (the father of that stillborn baby) whose family didn't approve of his marrying her, but at last they do, and he does. His mother can't argue with Mary's success. Eventually, "They all four of them were successful enough in their living" (260).

Pages 261–314 | This story told (and retold), the text shifts to the Hersland governesses again, first enumerating them as "a foreign woman, and a tall blond foreign american who later married a baker, and then Madeleine Wyman who was with them when Mrs. Hersland had in her living, her most important feeling" (260). Now we will have their stories, and we begin with Martha, the foreign woman. She is a "good musician" with, according to our matter-of-fact narrator, very little stupid being and almost no queerness in her, though it was hard to tell because no one got close to her (261). A governess since she was twenty, the now forty-year-old Martha has been in the States for ten years. She came because, after their parents died, she wanted her younger sister to become a teacher "in American where life would be easier" (261). But, "**She herself did not like it in America she wanted to go back to her old living where people spoke french**
(237) **and german and where it was natural for her to be a musician.**" Not so much in Gossols. So, Martha gets her sister established, stays "not very long" with the Herslands, and leaves. Intending to return to Europe, she somehow gets stuck in Ohio on the way out. "She stayed there and she gave music

lessons and she never got any further and she stayed there always until she died there, and she never had left America" (261). Meanwhile her vague younger sister, Olga, stays in Gossols teaching. They never spend time with one another again, as neither is willing to travel to see the other, and Olga, twenty years younger than Martha, "was afraid of her sister" (262).

The text then analyzes "The Foreign Woman" Martha for a few more pages, establishing that she was pretty balanced in her dependent independent being, and that "There was just enough queerness in her to hold her together" (263). "As I was saying," she was a good musician, and foreign, which is what Mr. Hersland wanted in a governess for his children at the time so, "**Theoretically, she was important to him, really she had no existence for him.**" After she left, none of the Herslands feel a great (264)
loss, but Mr. Hersland then "thought it was better that the children should have american training," not french and german, not music. They needed "strength and gymnastics and out of door living and swimming and shooting" (264). Mr. Hersland loses focus soon after, as he often does, and forgets about his plans for his children's education. Though he hardly notices when Martha leaves, he later expresses anger at the kids because they don't know French and German (269).

For some reason, though, the Hersland family stays in touch with Olga—"Everybody called her Olga. It was natural to be familiar with her" (265). Mr. Hersland finds her attractive, which comes as no surprise as our narrator claims that "she was round and pleasant and men liked her" (265). Because of that, "no one would ever naturally think of her as a spinster"; but that is, in fact, her nature, and, after lots of repeating, we learn it's what she becomes.

With the promise of more stories about Olga ahead ("as Alfred Hersland came to make fun of her, as Martha Hersland came to know her"), we move on to that tall blond woman with "no queerness in her," who eventually marries a baker (266). Though she was a healthy person, "**Stupid being was the whole of her. . . . It was just all of her.**" Our narrator (266)
reminds us, again, that "every one has in them their kind of stupid being," in their way of "loving, or working, or waking, or resting, or doing nothing, or having pleasant or angry feeling in them, or succeeding or failing" (267).

But, we see, the blond governess got more than her share of stupid. She didn't spend time reading and had only an "ordinary education," but Mr. Hersland wanted "a big healthy woman" who "knew all about farming" (269). This one fit the bill. The baker, her husband, was also big and blond, so they had a lot in common. Together they had kids, and she became bigger and grimier as the years passed. Only Mr. Hersland stayed in touch with her, dropping by "to see her and to eat a cake while he talked to her" (269). Sometimes the baker gave the Hersland children cream puffs, but this governess "was not important ever to the children" (270).

We now diverge from studying the governesses to ponder Mr. Hersland again. We learn more about what he was experiencing during this time in Gossols, how "then some women were attractive to him" but, to him, "it was a joke" (272). Each governess, in her turn, fits Mr. Hersland's ideal, but "mostly it was not a need in him" in the beginning of his middle living when his wife "was existent to him" (273). We learn that "later what was now an attraction to him would be then a need in him, later there will be a history of him" (273), another one of the text's encouraging cues to keep reading for what's ahead—perhaps some scandal! This diversion then wanders off into a contemplation of kinds of loving, then to types of women, revisiting Mrs. Hersland's background of "Bridgeport living," and finally landing on Madeleine Wyman.

A telling paragraph segues from Fanny Hersland's "eastern living" to "romance" (repeated six times) to Madeleine Wyman, who "owned the romance of their mother's early living" (278). This relationship was later "a sore feeling" in the children, because Madeleine came "to own their mother and their father, to them" (278). For the years that Madeleine was "living in the house with her," Fanny had her strongest sense of "important being in her." The Hersland children later recognize that, as they found their mother less central to their lives, as their father was "brushing people away from around him," Fanny was becoming "herself to herself in her" with Madeleine Wyman. These insights are followed by a paragraph about the "many ways of loving," and the narrator's direction that "this is now a history of" the third governess, followed by "this is now a history of the two of them"—Fanny Hersland and Madeleine Wyman (279).

Something is going on here, something Stein never overtly states but repeatedly hints at in the remaining thirty pages of this section, as we delve into the life of the third governess and her family, examine her relationship with the Hersland family, and dance around her influence over Mrs. Hersland. The text repeats what we now know (from much repeating) that Mrs. Hersland was not important to her children, "excepting to begin them," and repeats often that "Madeleine Wyman owned their mother . . . entirely," thereby making them feel like "something was cut off from them" (280).

We learn that Madeleine possessed a combination of the qualities of the first two governesses, that "she had everything" (283). She wasn't pretty, but she wasn't ugly either, and Mr. Hersland liked the conversations he had with her; he found her intelligent (which definitely means he liked her because she listened to him). Notably, we briefly revisit Mr. Hersland's character here; he "could be a coward in his living" and his children "told it to him" (284). We also observe, again, his penchant to advise people about what to do with their lives—the way he tells the second governess "whether she was getting fatter or thinner" and "gave advice to her about how to keep in condition" (285). Though he liked talking with/at Madeleine, "it was not a personal feeling" (286). But to Mrs. Hersland, "she was very personal"; "They had then for each other these two women very important being." (286)

We're also told about Madeleine's whole "foreign american" family, with four children and two living parents disconnected from one another by different levels of foreignness (287-88). Madeleine and her three younger siblings, Louise, Frank, and Helen, didn't know much about their parents' inner being or bottom natures since, according to the (always opinionated) narrator, parents are completely foreign subject matter to kids. And yet, years later, the Hersland children come to understand those parents, now long gone, by understanding each other:

> "They never however any one of them, the three Hersland children came to any realization of them until later they remembered them and reconstructed them and realised them and then reconstructed and realised the foreign parents from a reconstruction from their reconstructed children." (288)

The dramatic part of this story, though, is when Madeleine's family insists that she marry a rich man (whom she does marry, eventually), but she prefers to stay with the Herslands, a choice Mrs. Hersland encourages by doubling her wages and getting her a fancy dress made by Mary and Mabel. Promises are made here—about Madeleine's eventual marriage to the wealthy John Summers and their adopting then giving up a daughter, about the lives of Madeleine's siblings, Louise and Frank and Helen, and the long life of her mother, Mrs. Wyman—and then a reminder of what we're doing together: "**There is always then repeating, there is always then in every one beginning and ending, there is always then in every one stupid being, there is always then sometime some one to every one who ever was or is or will**
(291) **be living who knows the being in that one.**" In revisiting and retelling these stories, in repeatedly reconstructing these characters, we aim to know "the being in that one." And the promised details follow. We learn more about Louise, Frank, and Helen and their respective natures. We discover that John took on the task of "choosing and adopting" a girl, but then "sent her back to the home from where they had gotten her" (298). Turns out, they loved to travel, and Madeleine "had not wanted the child with her." Madeleine prefers traveling to motherhood. She is faithful to John and he to her, and they live a happy, financially wealthy life until he dies of a vague, unexplained illness.

"Later on there will be more" becomes another repeated refrain here, as the narrator urges readers forward. But we also circle back frequently ("as I was saying" and "to begin again"), enumerating the three governesses, reviewing the natures of the Herslands and Wymans, cataloging the types of being—dependent, independent, efficient, fighting, and resisting. As we near the end of this section, Mrs. Hersland and Madeleine Wyman begin to meld, with Madeleine taking on Fanny's qualities, her "Bridgeport living," after Fanny dies. In the end, "it is clear, the kind of being Mrs. Hersland had in her and which Madeleine Wyman had in her. More and more it was surer that this kind of describing leads to complete understanding of men and women" (312).

The section ends with the narrator reaffirming the practice of repeating: "**Slowly every one in continuous repeating, to their minutest variation, comes to be**

clearer to some one. . . . Slowly every kind of one comes into ordered recognition." (313)
And here, after nearly 300 pages, they remind us we have come to "an ending of the beginning of the history of the Hersland family" and we are about to set out on "a beginning of a description of the being and the living in each of the three Hersland children." We will start with Martha and "every one she ever knew in her living" (314).

"To begin then" (314).

MARTHA HERSLAND

Pages 315–419 | We want to take a minute here to pause and recognize that this style of storytelling can sometimes be tedious. If you're reading along, you already know this, and, believe us, we've been there; we get it. But there is certainly a theory behind this style and a clarity of purpose in its execution. We find that following this larger project, making sense of Stein's modernist novel-making, propels us forward, more even than the circuitous Hersland family plot can. Given that, the metafictional and suggestively autobiographical passage that begins the "Martha Hersland" section is compelling. It is one of those moments when the personality of the story-teller, that sometimes frustrating but always engaging narrator, becomes the most interesting part of the novel.

"I am writing for myself and strangers," the narrator reveals. "This is the only way that I can do it. Everybody is a real one to me, everybody is like some one else too for me. No one of them that I know can want to know it and so I write for myself and strangers." Because no one the narrator know cares about (317)
these things—they don't want to hear that "they are like many others"—our narrator has to write for the strangers who will get it. "No one who knows me can like it. At least they mostly do not like it that every one is a kind of men and women and I see it" (317).

But this peculiar perception of types, this "looking and comparing and classifying," is not a burden to our narrator: "There are many that I know and they know it. They are all of them repeating and I hear it. I love it and I tell it, I love it and now I will write it" (317). The joy in this

passage is infectious. "I love it and I write it," they tell us again. "Always more and more I love repeating, it may be irritating to hear from them but always more and more I love it of them. More and more I love it of them, the being in them, the mixing in them, the repeating in them, the deciding the kind of them every one
(317) is who has human being."

Now they will write it. And later, "there will be much more of it." And so there is. For the nearly 100 pages that follow this introduction the narrator outlines the process of writing a book like this one, the observing, listening, classifying and clarifying, the effort toward understanding as they work toward the ultimate goal of writing "the complete history of every one, the fundamental character of every one, the bottom nature in them, the mixtures in them, the strength and weakness of everything they have inside them, the flavor of them, the meaning in them, the being in them, and then you have a whole history then of each one" (318).

We recognize the narrative voice from the previous sections as they state the justifications for repetition with familiar meanderings of their own—the being in them, the bottom nature, the "as I was saying." Only in paying attention to the "steady sounding" of each person, often over years of knowing them, can we come to know their natures, the narrator argues. Listening carefully, "Each one slowly comes to be a whole one to me.
(331) Each one slowly comes to be a whole one in me." That internalization—from *to* me to *in* me—is an important shift, central to the narrator's project and, we propose, to Stein's thinking about what a novel can do.

It will come as no surprise that each of the narrator's observations are repeated over and over in this first hundred pages of the "Martha Hersland" section. The delightful addition, however, is the reminder that the narrator loves this work—making it live, making it their own. "There are many that I know and they know it. They are all of them repeating and I hear it. More and more I understand it. I love it and I tell it. I love it and always I will
(319) write it."

This work is not so obviously delightful for the reader, however. It is at this almost plot-free point in the text where the going gets nearly impossibly tedious, where you may need something to buoy you up and urge you onward. It seems that the narrator expects this will be intellectually curiosity about human nature, how diverse and yet how predictably similar we all are. It's in most of our natures to "love repeating," to notice and follow patterns. "Loving repeating is in a way earth feeling. Some children have loving repeating for little things and story-telling . . . Slowly this comes out in them in all their children being, in their eating, playing, crying, and laughing" (323). Following patterns, then, is human, a shared capability that we see in most children and that ("as I was saying") is "the beginning of learning the complete history of every one" (328). And so we return to classification of types—resisting, winning, attacking, fighting, bottom natures, and so on . . . and on.

Surprisingly, the now very present and self-conscious narrator guides us through these pages, with constant reminders of their companionship in this endeavor—"I am thinking and feeling"; "I am hearing, feeling, seeing"; "I was listening, feeling, looking"; "every one is puzzling to me"; and, of course, "as I was saying." The repetition of the mantra "There are many that I know and I know it" leads us through the process of understanding "the kinds of men and women." The narrator knows this work is hard; they get that the novel has quite likely become wearisome. Even they "sometimes . . . get a little tired of it, mostly I am always ready to do it, always I love it" (333). The lessons on how this work of understanding is accomplished become overt, such as this one on listening: "Listening to repeating is often irritating, listening to repeating can be dulling, always repeating is all of living, everything in a being is always repeating, always more and more listening to repeating gives to me completed understanding. Each one slowly comes to be a whole one to me. Each one slowly comes to be a whole one in me" (335).

"Each one slowly comes to be a whole one *to me*. Each one slowly comes to be a whole one *in me*" [emphasis added]: This phrase is repeated more than ten times in the space of three pages (334-336), then with variation for a few pages more. Because the story here is "the description of my learning. Then there will be a beginning again of Martha Hersland and her being and her living," we are led to understand that this repetitive work is equally important as the Hersland plot (337). In this Martha section, it is half the story. And because understanding people is a slow process, this section, engaging in that process, must move at a similar, sometimes irritating, pace. "As I have said in writing, often," the narrator repeats, "for many years someone is baffling, the repeated hearing of them does not make the completed being they have in them to anyone" (347).

But with careful listening, the whole of a person's being can be accessed, and with some it's easier than with others, who are "a puzzle." The narrator reminds us several times that "it takes many years of hearing the repeating in one before the whole being is clear to the understanding of one who has it as being to love repeating" (351). The narrator is fully present throughout these pages, referencing their process, even being self-congratulatory about their insight: "**There are many that I know and I know it. They are repeating always the whole of them and I understand it. They are, each**
(353) **one then, sometime a whole one to me. I know it and I tell it.**" Learning, knowing, and telling are then enumerated and explored. The narrator describes how "knowing" evokes various feelings—from "a sense of being filled up" (354), a "serious solemn filling inside me" (355), to being "quietly there in me" (354), to being "disturbed" (354) and then how knowing becomes telling in similarly various forms—sometimes "bursting out," sometimes slowly or sharply, "sometimes it comes very repeatingly, sometimes very willingly out of me" (358).

The metafictional narrator then explores this process through "this one" and "that one," highlighting similarities and differences in their quest for a complete history "of this one in some one, perhaps never really inside anyone" (361). The idea that everyone is particular yet also typical pervades these pages, concluding with these three sentences, set apart in two distinctively short paragraphs:

> **Everybody is a real one to me, everybody is like some one else too to me.**
>
> **Everybody has their own being in them. Every one is a kind of men and**
> (365) **women.**

These last two sentences are repeated, word for word and conceptually, as the narrator transitions to groupings of types, because "each one must be a whole one, each one must be to some one like some one else, like some other one" (366).

But before we go on, we backpedal a bit to "a little description" of learning, of kinds and types, "of the learning of knowing of the kinds there are of men and women, of the resembling that makes the kinds of them around one" (368). Learning is the center that these observations spiral from, as the narrator repeatedly "begins again" toward understanding. Seeing resemblances, recognizing kinds, and "knowing is interesting, defining, confusing, uncertain and certain." Resemblances multiply and repeat until, recognizing similarities, they "fall into an ordered system" (373). The narrator arrives at a moment of confidence and clarity:

> I do know very much of the being in men and women. I do know very many of them. I do know the resemblances in the and the kinds of them, the divisions into kinds of them that is important for the understanding of them. I do know many of them, I know them, I understand, I explain them, they are themselves then to me, they are whole ones to me, I know it and I tell it, I know it more and more and more and more I tell it. (374)

They then begin to enumerate how the resemblances come together, with attention, again, to the "bottom nature" present in each person. With humorous sexual innuendo, the narrator explains, "This bottom in them in some can be solid, in some frozen, in some thinner, slimier, drier, very dry and not so dry and in some a stimulation entering into the surface of the mass that is them to make an emotion does not get into it, the mass then that is them, to be swallowed up in it to be emerging, in some it is swallowed up and never then is emerging" (376). Paragraph after paragraph they develop "groupings" of men and women, based on natures and kinds, revisiting ways of being.

Several times the narrator appears to simplify the groupings into "two general kinds." But those two kinds change from only "the attacking kind" and the "the resisting kind" (377) to "all extremes of these two kinds" melding with dependence and independence, and "very very many mixings in every one of some of all the kinds of them" (379). For a bit of comic relief, we call your attention to a sentence we all enjoyed for its concrete "substance" language:

> There must now be then more description of the way each one is made of a
> substance common to their kind of them, thicker, thinner, harder, softer, all
> of one consistency, all of one lump, or little lumps stuck together to make a
> whole one cemented together sometimes by the same kind of being sometimes
> by other kind of being in them, some with lump vegetablish or wooden or
> (378) metallic in them.

You're welcome. And by the way, comic relief is an appropriate interaction. We're convinced Stein keeps us amused on purpose.

After a few pages spent analyzing "the resisting kind," we enter another moment of metafictionality where the narrator reflects on how difficult it is to write about this stuff. "I am all unhappy in this writing," they reveal. I get it, they tell us; I'm just not sure how to help you get it, so (what else?) let's "begin again with telling it." And here the language becomes physical again; attacking being is not "an earthy kind of substance" but of "a pulpy not dust not dirt" texture that "can be slimy, gelatinous, gluey, white opaquy kind of thing" (383). Because it's not clear to the narrator yet, they will write more about it until it is—and here the verbs shift to present perfect progressive with what they know blending with what they are learning in the moment, from "I know" to "I am thinking" to "I am saying" to "I know" again (384).

This, too, is where our favorite kind of being first appears—"the slow, stupid, gelatinous being" as the narrator begins to connect types with actual characters (387). One person the narrator observes "had in her to be muggily resisting except when some one was engulfing her" (383). Another person is, like Napolean, "to themselves unchanging, having a destiny from the beginning" (394).[2] The process of understanding, of puzzling

2. If the narrator is enumerating characters in Stein's world, this Napoleonic person might very well be, as he often was in Stein's writing, Picasso. A few pages later a person with attacking being "with a good head on him" is linked with Herbert Spencer, the poet (365).

out kinds, is often slow, the narrator reminds us again, but they're doing it *right now*. "More and more I would like to make it clear to some one how I see men and women, how I see kinds in men and women" (396). With repeated effort, revisiting various characteristics, beginning again and again, it's coming together. **"I know a great deal then and I tell it now when I am still puzzling."** One character "for many years was baffling to me" the (397)
narrator confesses, "for a long long time I was puzzling and puzzling" over him. A difficult case of "one with a passion for being loving" and "a fixed scheme of living for grace and beauty" who "is a clear one to me" now (402). Still, he gets pages of attention, as the narrator carefully studies his characteristics in their repetition—rationalism, opportunism, passion, a love of luxury and beauty. This character suggests her brother Leo or David Hersland. But, to be truthful, it's not clear through the final pages of this section if the narrator is describing one person or several. They reference "finishing up with this one," of "this one coming to be a whole one inside me," but then they begin again with the same characteristics, the same language of "puzzling" and "baffling" of "experiencing beauty" and "affection for luxury" (405). In several instances, they reference "these ten of this kind" (405-6) and "the fifth one of the six that I am now describing" (409).

As this section ends with the promise to "begin again the history of Martha Hersland and of every one she ever knew in living," it also re-centers the characters of men and women in their childhood experiences because some "are whole ones in them when they are little ones some when they are young ones, when they are beginning their living, than they are any other time in their living" (419). A childhood incident illustrating this point follows the promise to trace Martha's character from her beginning: **"One little girl, one little boy, some one, many do something to a little girl who does not like it, she shows just then no sign of reacting to it, the little girl who does not like it."** The fallout from this on the girl's character suggests the (416)
direction Martha's life will take: "The little one shows no feeling, the little one then is not remembering, the little one then does some violent thing to the one that has done the thing the little one was not liking," pretty clearly suggesting the pattern of denial. repression and acting out that

often follows an incident of childhood sexual violence. "As I was saying, this is often happening" (416), the narrator notes.

The larger task at hand, however, doesn't change as we move through a break in the narrative: "Always there will be here writing a description of all the kinds of ways there can be seen to be kinds of men and women" (414).

Pages 420–524 | Following the (rare) page break, the narrator confronts their readers' possible waning interest: "**Sometimes some one is very interesting to some one, very, very interesting to some one and then that one comes together to be a whole one and then that one is not any more, at all, interesting to the one**
(420) **knowing that one, that one then is shrunken by being a whole one.**" But what, they query, could be more tantalizing than this wholeness that "is very interesting" (421). They proceed, again, to describe different kinds of human wholeness in funny, common language as "little lumps of one kind of being held together or separated from each other" and as "a mushy mass with a skin to hold them in and so make one [a whole]" (421).

One particular mushy mass of a person becomes the focus of the next few pages, as the narrator keeps promising to get to Martha Hersland. This unnamed person and Martha are both "independent dependent kind of them" and, in fact, both could apply or refer to Martha Hersland, but there is a point to be made first about individuals as types (422). This person is a type, an independent dependent with attacking being, a mass of resisting "that was mostly all stupid being" (425). She is "like many very many men and women . . . like all of them that have in them independent dependent being" and yet she is also an individual, "different from all the others of them for this one had her own skin and so was separated from all of them that have in them that have or had or will have the same kind of being" (426). Recognizing the type is like "**Knowing a map and then seeing the place and knowing then that the roads actually existing are like the map, to**
(428) **some is always astonishing and always then very gratifying.**"

The description of Martha begins, finally, with an incident from when she was little ("just beginning her schooling") and running in a muddy street behind others who "had run ahead to get home and they had left her." She was angry, dragging an umbrella and threatening to throw it in the mud. But nobody heard her. "'I have throwed the umbrella in the mud' burst from her, she had thrown the umbrella in the mud and that was the end of it all in her" (426). This incident characterizes Martha, but is not yet recognizable as definitive of her kind of being; "filled full of angry feeling, with despairing feeling, with responsible feeling, with frightened feeling, no one then could be very certain of the kind of being Martha had in her" (427-8). Childhood behaviors like this sometimes become like the maps to character for people as they age, the narrator tells us. Some kinds of being are apparent in children, and some don't become apparent until their "middle living."

The narrator then ruminates about children and how unpredictable they are, how their behaviors don't always reveal their nature: "Children are confusing and deceiving to many," we learn (431). And yet, that incident with Martha and the umbrella comes to be a touch point for understanding her—"her anger and resentment and desperation" and her "triumphing" as she carries out her threat and throws the umbrella in the mud. "Martha Hersland did this and she was a little girl then and slowly now there will come to be a complete description of the nature in her that this I have been just describing does not now help very much to be understanding" (433).

Again, we are reminded, it is in repetition of behaviors that people truly reveal themselves. So the description of Martha will encompass "how everyone knowing Martha felt the being in her" (434); seeing Martha through the children she grows up with (in the small houses), through "governesses and the servants and her brothers and her teachers and her mother and her father and later other girls and boys and later her lover and later her husband and very many who then knew her and then again her brothers and her father, and again then everybody who then and on from then to her ending knew her" (434) will be how we access Martha as an individual and a type.

Paragraphs follow exploring Martha's being and her wholeness, her independent dependence, her relationship with various governesses, and her affinity for the poor people around her. We also learn that she was

"to no one quite entirely pleasing, but most of those knowing her then like her well enough whenever they thought about her and sometimes then they did not like her" (447). This passage, too, gets repeated, as we examine how others feel about Martha, particularly her father. David also "had in him independent dependent being," just as his daughter did, but they were very different—and the narrator promises to help us see how (449). Because his daughter is "never very interesting to him," Mr. Hersland fails to notice their similar being. "His feeling was very different with his
two sons who each in their way were annoying to him but Martha was annoying
(451) to him being as she was of the same kind of being as the being that was in him."

The text also suggests that Martha has a rather awkward first sexual experience with the son of one of the poor people—"the little boy who with his sister lived with the father who smoked to help his asthma" (454). He "wanted her to do loving . . . but this was not very much of a success" (454). Martha is too nervous, not very daring, and "a little like being afraid of everything, a little like a very stupid way of being" (454). A few pages later the narrator repeats that the two of them had had a go at loving, at doing "things they should not be doing," and though Martha didn't resist, "it could not come to anything for there was not in her anything really active inside her then" (458). Also, she just isn't very interesting; the people around her know very little about her, easily forget her, and often don't include her, even though she is "completely of them the people living near the Hersland family then, she was then not of the living of her father and her mother" (456).

This brings back the tantalizing clue that "Something happened to her then that made her for now a little time more than the whole one she was all her living to herself . . . it was really just a little accentuation of being put in motion and of that I will now give a very little description" (455). Of course, no description follows. And Martha doesn't tell anyone anything, but "something" clearly happened to her that "made all her being move together and faster than it had ever had motion before in her" (455). This something is hinted at then pinned down as "seeing a man hitting a woman with an umbrella in another part of town." This resulted in her "consequent deciding to go to college and get that kind of education"

(455). That umbrella: is it one of Stein's coded words for sexuality? Abuse? Oppression? At the very least, it's a narrative connector, a motif.

"To begin then," the narrator inserts, then moves on to the moment when Martha stops being quiet and starts to become fed up with her father's anger. It is when the governess Madeleine Wyman (she's back!) is "beginning to take charge of her," and Martha begins to resist her, because she fears her governess more than she fears her father. Madeleine was "a compacted power that kept going and always was there" (457). Martha first rejects her father's command that she learn housekeeping, though she is always "studying in one way or another" (460). Mostly we learn, repeatedly, that Martha "was not then really very interesting to any one" (455, 456, 457, 458, 460 . . .). The narrator compares her solid being with "that other one the first one I was describing" whose substance "sort of bobbled up and down in her" and made her "a heavy slightly sticky one" with a dull kind of obstinacy (461). Not so with Martha who was full of strong emotion, despite being so solid.

Martha's affinity for the people around her "in very small houses" comes to be a problem when many of them get older and start working. Though she is with them in feeling, they are divided "by the future living that would be different in her living from the future living any of them would naturally be having" (464). The only time to spend together, then, is in the evenings, and her father begins to find her gadding about at night "inappropriately"—"that was no way a daughter of his in his position should be acting"—even though he spends his Sundays with the very same people, "sat down in the houses with the women when they were cooking and ate something there in the kitchen with them" (465). He wants Martha to be different, to be "the kind of educated person that it was right he should have for a daughter" (466).

Thank goodness, then, for that elusive "real attacking moment" that leads her to higher education (466). That moment takes shape a bit more in its return here, as the narrator adds detail:

> . . . one day when she was alone in another part of the town where she had gone to take a lesson in singing she saw a man hit a woman with an umbrella,

> and the woman had a red face partly in anger and partly in asking and the man wanted the woman to know then that he wanted her to leave him alone then in a public street where people were passing and Martha saw this and this man was for her the ending of living I have been describing that she had been living. She would go to college, she knew it then and understand everything and know the meaning of the living and the feeling in men and
> (467) women.

While we are learning about Martha, the narrator persistently reminds us that she has "trouble in her living" ahead, that eventually she goes to college, meets her husband, then leaves her husband and returns to live with her father. "It will come out clearly" how and why this happens, they promise, but first "there will be a little more description of her daily living" (467). Plot spoiled, readers can better focus on the whys rather than the whats. The text also name drops a couple of boyfriends—Harry Brenner, who was one of the poor people (and probably the one she did things she shouldn't be doing with); John Davidson, who was more "appropriately" of her social class; and Phillip Redfern who becomes her husband.

The two umbrella incidents that express and develop Martha's character reappear several times with a few additional insights as repetition unfolds. The narrator tells us that these incidents cause "a shock of commotion in her" so strong that it gives her life direction. "As I was saying that happened once to her when she was a very little one when she threw down the umbrella, it happened every now and then in her, it happened, as I was saying, when she saw the man hitting the woman in the street with his umbrella to rid himself then of
(469) her and of the asking in her."

Here the narrative shifts noticeably in tone and becomes more traditional in its storytelling. "This is now to be more history of her and how she came to have a lover and how he came to marry her and how he came to leave her and what happened then to him and what happened then to her" (469). Referencing the long tradition of the novel as *roman* or romance (see our Introduction), it is fascinating that, in the section focused on the woman character, at the moment when she is choosing a husband and marrying, it is at this point where the narrative becomes most traditional.

Here it moves away from the experimental modernist novel Stein has been constructing, particularly in the previous, increasingly plot-free section. There are more periods and more simple subject-verb-object sentences interspersed with the now familiar rambling repetitive passages (about, for example, how "astonishing" it is that one person sees things differently from others). Here also, on pages 429–440, Stein includes a revised version of her earlier work, the more traditional novella *Fernhurst* (See our exploration of this in "The Continuous Making of *TMOA*," Chapter Five.)

The story begins with Phillip Redfern, the Darcy to Martha's Elizabeth, who is a construct of the American West, a rebellious son, a champion of "liberty, equality, opportunity, beauty, feeling, for all women" (472); in an earlier version of Stein's *Fernhurst* he was called "A Student of the Nature of Woman" in the subtitle. He is, in short, a romantic hero. At least at first. In him, the opposing forces of his parents' influence battle it out—the domineering, reserved father and the "strong enthusiasm of emotion of his mother's nature" (473). He is a keen observer of the "constant spectacle of an armed neutrality between his parents," a reader and a thinker, with "wonderful dreams" and "much real emotion of sympathising" (474). When he goes away to school it is to a "typical coeducational college of the west, a completely democratic institution" where no one cared who your grandfather was "no one was held responsible for the father they had" (475):

> This democracy was really almost complete among all of them and included very simple comradeship among them all, all of the men and women there together then. The men were mostly simple, direct and earnest in their relations with the women there being educated with them, the men, most of them treating them with generosity and kindliness enough and never really doubting even for a moment their right to any learning or occupation the women, any of them were able to acquire then. (475)

Among the comrades he meets there is Martha Hersland, "a blond good-looking young woman full of moral purpose and educational desires" (and this is the most concise physical description readers have of her in all the looping, reiterative "Martha Hersland" section of this novel). They soon single one another out from the crowd in a way that "was all new, strange and dangerous for the south-western man and all perfectly simple and matter of course for the western girl" (476).

The suggestive Victorian language of sexuality pervades here as "their intercourse steadily grew more constant and familiar," and they go out in the country "plunging vigorously through the snow . . . excited with their own health and their youth and the freedom" (476). They spend three years together like this, with him "discoursing of his life and aims, she listening, understanding and sympathising." There is one jealous moment reported when John Davidson's visiting younger brother puts his head in Martha's lap *right in front of Phillip* who complains and is corrected by honest, forthright Martha. And then, as if in the margins or between the paragraphs, they are married, and she becomes "Mrs. Redfern."

From the start, it's not a promising union, as they move beyond happily-ever-after, and Redfern begins exhibiting "elaborate chivalry" while "their minds and natures were separated by great gulfs" (477). If his parents demonstrated "an armed neutrality among equals" what he found in Martha was "an inferior who could not learn the rules of the game" (477). As for Martha:

> *Mrs. Redfern* never understood what had happened to her. In a dazed blind way she tried all ways of breaking through the walls that confined her. She threw herself against them with impatient energy and again she tried to destroy them piece by piece. She was always thrown back bruised and dazed and never quite certain whence came the blow and how it was dealt or why. It was a long agony, she never became wiser or more indifferent, she struggled on always in the same dazed eager way.

(477)

This devastating portrait of a marriage, of the enforced disappearance of a woman into the life of her husband and the suggestion of physical violence, only gets more painful in the pages that follow, as Redfern earns his doctoral degree in philosophy, accepting a position as department chair at Farnham, a women's college. There he encounters "two interesting personalities . . . the dean, Miss Charles and her friend Miss Dounor" (478). The use of the word "interesting" here is foreboding, considering the earlier repeated refrain that Martha was not interesting to anyone. When Hannah Charles invites the new professor to tea to meet the faculty, we are told he enters alone.

Our attention shifts with his to these two women, the dean who is the daughter and granddaughter of remarkable women, and her companion, who "was possessed of a sort of transfigured innocence which made a deep impression on the vigorous practical mind of Miss Charles who while keeping her completely under her control was nevertheless in awe of her blindness to worldly things and of the intellectual power of her clear sensitive mind" (479). The classic intellectual woman, protected and otherworldly, Miss Cora Dounor immediately attracts Redfern. They have an auspicious first encounter, with him looking "with interest at this new presentment of gentleness and intelligence who greeted him with awkward shyness" and her losing her self-consciousness "during this eager discussion" (479-80).

Then, "in the height of the discussion, there came up to them a blond, eager, good-looking young woman whom Redfern observing presented as his wife to his new acquaintance." Awkward! Miss Dounor is immediately flustered and says, "Mrs. Redfern yes yes, of course, your wife I had forgotten," and then she is left speechless. "Mrs. Redfern" nervously encourages them to go on talking, and then the three of them continue, with Miss Dounor "fixed on Redfern's face and her tall constrained body filled with eagerness," Redfern paying equal "courteous deference" to both women, and "Mrs. Redfern her blond good-looking face filled with eager anxiety to understand listened to one and then the other with the same anxious care." (480)

The narrator intones, then, for a few paragraphs about how fateful the twenty-ninth year is in the transition to adulthood, particularly in "our american life" where we aren't forced into adult choices until we're thirty. At thirty "we find at last that vocation for which we feel ourselves fit and to which we willingly devote continued labor" (481). Redfern, after trying several other paths, had come to the point in his life "for the decisive influence in his career" (481), and that influence is Miss Dounor.

Plot dominates here in what feels at first like a refreshing break from experimentation, but comes to read as a brief, old-fashioned, sentimental vignette. We get a vivid account of Redfern's drift away from Martha toward Cora Dounor, "a spirit so delicate so free so gentle and intelligent that no severity of suffering could deter him from seeking the exquisite knowledge that this companionship could give him"; we also observe "this awkward reserved woman" progress through her "slow growth of interest to admiration and then to love" (482). But unlike in the typical American novel, the text favors the extra-marital relationship for what the narrator calls a "french habit" of cultivating joy. From this perspective, Martha's sturdy American morality gets in the way. "She tried resolutely to interpret it all in terms of comradeship and great equality of intellectual interests never admitting to herself for a moment the conception of a possible marital disloyalty" until she is forced into realization not by the "hard wall of courtesy that Redfern had erected before her" but by the intervention of an angry Miss Charles. The dean calls Martha out ("I think you understand quite well," she says of the gossip that surrounds them) then insists that Mrs. Redfern intervene (483).

The intervention is the point. Miss Charles is seeking a showdown (see our discussion of lesbian subtexts in Chapter Four). And now that Martha knows, she has to act, and in order to act, she has to watch her husband carefully, "she must gain the knowledge she dreaded to possess," the knowledge that would prove him deceitful and dishonorable (484). She finds proof, finally, in a letter he leaves on his desk: "She read it to the end, she had her evidence" (484). And for the remainder of this section (thirty-five more pages) we study the outcome of these few pages of plot, as we scrutinize the motivations and self-deceptions, the kinds of being that lead people to do what they do. The narrator signals this return by spinning out from the letter and how heavy it is with both meaning and emptiness, and with an emphatic "As I was saying."

What do words mean when meanings can change so profoundly, when people's very characters can be read so differently, the narrator asks. "Now to begin again with what I know of the being in Phillip Redfern, now to begin again a description of Phillip Redfern and always now I will be using words having in

my feeling, thinking, imagining very real meaning." Redfern sees himself—and (485)
continues to the end to see himself—as "completely chivalrous, completely a gentleman" (486). Here the narrator also references four others by name—A. Johnson, Frank Hackart, Mary Helbing, and Sarah Sands—who all credit their good qualities with leading them into bad things. And the bad things are, then, not their fault. All of them, including Redfern, "have it in common that in remembering anything they forget all the emotion they had then in them and so it must have been the other person's fault it happened, anything" (487). They see themselves, in other words, very differently from how others see them.

The way the novel fills out Redfern's character in these pages is intriguing, as realism is broken down to various perceptions in a modernist move Stein becomes famous for later, like a prose version of a Picasso painting or Duchamp's "Nude Descending a Staircase." Redfern, the narrator reports, was to most everyone "a man always failing in his living, and to Miss Dounor he was a saint among men and to Mrs. Redfern he was wonderful in the honorable courtesy in him and mostly every one sometime thought he was a bad man and mostly to every one he was a man given to lying." He thinks of (489)
himself as "a man simple, sensuous and passionate," a "literary man and sometimes a politician" (489). He is certainly a failure, but "he always struggles on, filled to the very end with hope and courage, always defeated and always ready to make a fresh assault" (490). This romantic self-deception, the narrator suggests, also characterizes Lord Byron and Oscar Wilde, as well as the aforementioned Johnson, Sands, Hackart and, they add, Melanctha, who is a central character in Stein's first published work, *Three Lives*, which appeared in 1909, just after she completed this novel. The final summation, this cubist paragraph, places the perception of Redfern variously in one impression:

> Phillip Redfern then had to himself a feeling of the being in him that was to him in a way a simple thing. Phillip Redfern was to Miss Dounor a man of saintly strength and courage and chivalrous feeling and self-sacrificing. Phillip Redfern was to Mrs. Redfern a man before whom she wanted to be intelligent, and honorable in acting and in feeling and

delicate, and to be pleasing by knowing Greek and naive realism. Phillip Redfern was to very many a man who was always lying. Phillip Redfern was to very many a very brilliant man gone altogether wrong. Phillip Redfern was to very many a man always wronging every one. Phillip Redfern was to many a very brilliant man and a very weak one. Phillip Redfern was to some the kind of man I have been just describing. This
(492-493) has now been a little history of him.

[Note: We have arranged the spacing as it appears in the 1995 Dalkey Archives edition with "Phillip Phillip Redfern Phillip Phillip Phillip" down the right side. See our Chapter Two on "The Modernist Sentence."]

After this discussion of Redfern (and not so much Martha), the narrator urges us to consider how people perceive of themselves as virtuous, of how they come to be certain about who they are, particularly when they are wrong: "Always more and more I want to know of each one what certainty means to them, how they come to be certain of anything, what certainty means to them and how contradiction does not worry them and how it does worry them and . . . what any one and every one means by anything they are saying" (494). They look again at Redfern's self-deception, then at Johnson and Hackart's, and concludes with their own doubt and errors: "Perhaps no one will ever know the complete history of every one. This is a sad thing" (499). But despite the "sadness and gentle melancholy despairing" our narrator has for their failures in understanding the complete history of every one, they can still find hope in repeating (454). "Repeating is what I am loving. Sometimes there is in me a sad feeling for all the repeating no one loving repeating is hearing. It is like any beauty that no one is seeing, it is a
(500) lovely thing . . ."

While promising a tour of the feelings of Redfern's three women, the narrator keeps interrupting their narrative with moments of self-doubt and self-revelation. Paragraphs begin with "I am thinking" and "I am beginning," then "As I am saying," and are interrupted with "It is hard telling" and "it is hard to know" until, finally, they give up on the women altogether and give in to self doubt: "Always now I am despairing. It is a

> very melancholy feeling I have in me now I am despairing about really knowing the complete being of any one of each of these three of them Miss Dounor and Miss Charles and Mrs. Redfern." (504)

But they wade back in, trying to figure out the distinctive types of being of all of the characters in this love triangle (quadrangle?), deciding who to blame, then concluding that "everybody is perfectly right" (507). They are all living true to their being, "right in their own living" in a way that takes courage (510). The narrator remarks on this courage, how hard it is "to buy bright colored handkerchiefs when every one having good taste uses white ones" or to buy a clock. "It is very hard to have the courage of your being in you, in clocks, in handkerchiefs, in aspirations, in liking things that are low, in anything" (510). Again, "It is a very difficult thing to have courage to buy clocks and handkerchiefs you are liking, you are seriously liking and everybody thinks then you are joking." (510)

The narrator has another go at the story, then, at what happens with the three women. Cora Dounor "was complete in her loving, she had complete understanding in desiring in all her relation with Phillip Redfern" and, at that time, was "completely succeeding in living" (512). Very little is said of what happens after the sheen wears off, when Redfern has to leave Farnham; the story leaps to when Miss Dounor becomes bitter "when Redfern was no longer existing in living" (513). Miss Charles keeps Miss Dounor with her for a while, but she "was not a nice one at all," and becomes more and more controlling after Dounor leaves her—presumably with Redfern. When Miss Charles was "not succeeding in keeping Miss Dounor with her," she comes out on top by "not having any remembrance in her of the trouble she had had with her" (513). She "went on always to her ending completely owning the college of Farnham" (516). The narrator has a lot to say about the kind of being in Miss Charles, and about the many others with similar "dependent independent" and "not nice" ways (516).

The sad story is Martha's/Mrs. Redfern's. Miss Dounor "made it very certain to everyone that Mrs. Redfern had no intelligence no understanding" until Martha has to confront her. Finally, the Redferns are forced to leave Farnham, and they "never lived anywhere together again" (512, 515).

Martha doesn't completely understand the scope of her situation, though. Expecting reconciliation, she goes off travelling and studying "and preparing herself to be a companion to him in intellectual living" (517). She never gives up hope that they will be together again, "studying and striving and travelling and working" until he dies young, "and then she knew they would not live together again" (517). She returns to the Hersland ten acres "where then her father and mother were living and her mother was weakening then a little while later she died there and Martha finished her living staying with her father who had then lost his great fortune" (517-18).

And that's the end of Martha Hersland's story. Or is it? The narrator promises more information to come "more description of Martha Hersland, Mrs. Redfern, written in the history of the ending of the living of Mr. David Hersland, her father, in the history of the living and the later living of her brother Alfred Hersland, in the history of her brother David Hersland and in the history of the ending of his living" (523-24). There is more to come of all the Herslands, whose lives are intertwined. These last few pages of the Martha Hersland section also reorient us to the continuous present of the novel. While Martha's marriage is unravelling, Alfred is about to marry Julia Dehning, and the narrator is preparing us for the next section: Alfred Hersland and Julia Dehning.

Part Two

[ALFRED HERSLAND AND JULA DEHNING]

Pages 528–660 | As we focus in on the second Hersland child in the Alfred and Julia section, the novel's style moves progressively away from the traditional storytelling we (occasionally) encountered in the Martha section. The narrative begins again (and doubles down on) shedding plot and character as this section becomes as much about writing and "the writer" as it is about this Hersland couple—a trend that will accelerate through the end of the novel. We also begin to see more visual experimentation, with the placement of words on the page and the arrangement of repeated phrases. The narrative incursions of self-doubt and loss of purpose also increase as the detours multiply and ruminations take over page after page. We begin, though, with a moment of assessment.

We have been learning "the history of a great many men and women" and sometime we will get "a history of all of the rest of them. This is pretty nearly certain" (528). So here, nearly 500 pages in, the narrator can't promise us what's coming, but it's becoming "pretty nearly certain." The larger task remains the same: to "give a history of every kind of men and women, every men and women." This portion will be "the complete history of Alfred Hersland and of every one he ever came to know in living" (528).

The narrator also gestures toward explaining the tone of the preceding

Martha section. "I want to know sometime all about sentimental feeling" and all the different ways people come to claim certainty, "and how contradiction does not worry them" (530). They hint that they have started writing another book with many other histories, many other explorations of types, but they will not continue it until they finish this history of the Herslands, beginning again with Alfred.

The narrator then riffs on certainty and how, "As I was saying virtuous feeling and being certain of anything is to me very interesting" (530). They explore varieties of certainty, of a built-up pile of little sure things, of dramatic arrangement of scenes of certainty, of comparative certainty, of certainty that loves company—because company keeps certainty "from freezing or melting or evaporating or in some way disappearing" (531). Some have it and lose it. Some have it intermittently. Some never have it. If only, the narrator concludes, they knew all the ways that people had certainty and virtuous feeling: "I would then be a very wise one to every one" (531).

But they are not there yet. Here, at the beginning of the Alfred section, it makes our narrator "a little unhappy" that so many things are still peculiar and strange to them. "**It does certainly make me a little unhappy**
(532) **that every one sometime is a queer one to me.**" And they repeat variations on this phrase—with "certainly," "unhappy," and "queer" in each iteration. Apparently, paying attention to people gets "depressing to any one of such of them that wants to be understanding the being in men and women" (533). The narrator's failure to achieve certainty, except in their awareness that people are funny/peculiar/strange/queer to them and sometimes even a little crazy, becomes "disillusioning."

The disillusionment of living, as the narrator calls it, happens when we realize that no one can ever completely agree with us, not really. And once we realize "this thing," it is "the beginning of being an old man or an old woman" (533). "**This is the real thing of disillusion that no one, not any one really is believing, seeing, understanding, thinking anything as you**
(533) **are thinking, believing, seeing, understanding such a thing.**" This is where the quest for certainty lands our narrator, and foreshadows what's ahead, i.e., less certainty, more disillusionment. In fact, the story that's ahead, of "the

younger son in the Hersland family . . . will be completely a history of the disillusionment of such realising and the dying then of that one, of young David Hersland then" (533).

Ah, but it's not just David. The narrator breaks in to remind us that they know whereof they speak. *They* know the "complete disillusionment" that comes from having nobody agree with you, and understanding, finally, that no one ever will, because "they can't change. The amount they agree is important to you until the amount they do not agree with you is completely realised by you" (535). Then, reiterating what they confessed 200 pages earlier, "you say you will write for yourself and strangers, you will be for yourself and strangers and this then makes an old man or an old woman of you" (535).

At this point we are several pages into this Alfred Hersland and Julia Dehning section, and there has been no mention of either Alfred or Julia since Alfred was introduced in the first paragraph with the promise of "a complete history" of his being. Twenty-four pages in there is another promise that "Alfred Hersland will soon then be interesting. There will soon be a description of him begun" (556). But for now, don't look for either Alfred or Julia. This section of the novel, in fact, has very little about Julia and scant new information about Alfred. There are two strains through these 118 pages before the next page break. One is a gathering and regathering of facts we already know about Alfred, mostly of his boyhood in Gossols. The other is a metafictional stream of insight and doubt, concerned mainly with the process of writing. The story twists these two strands throughout, but for clarity, we will begin by following the narrator through this section, and then return to review what we learn about Alfred.

The narrator goes confessional on us early, diving into what it takes to write a book like this, and revisiting those clocks and handkerchiefs that we like when no one else does. "It is always very difficult to like anything, to do anything," the narrator asserts, because "you write a book and while you write it you are ashamed for every one must think you are a silly or a crazy one and yet you write it and you are ashamed, you know you will be laughed at or pitied by every one and you have a queer feeling and you are not very certain and you go on writing." It is difficult to have the courage of your strange and (535) singular preferences, whatever they are; it is difficult to buy the clocks and handkerchiefs you love when everybody thinks you must be joking; it is difficult to write the experimental novel that compels you.

The narrator admits they probably aren't telling this in a way that makes sense, but assures the reader that they will explain it in more detail through their descriptions of other concepts. Then they repeat their ideas about repeating and being and certainty and the difficulties of liking what no one else likes. Sometimes this is "a difficult thing" and sometimes it's "a wonderful thing" (537). Or a mix. "It is a wonderful thing as I was saying and
(537) I am now repeating." There is so much repeating in life that the narrator is again surprised that others don't realize it. This repeating reveals the many types of men and women and how they differ morally and intellectually, which the narrator also promises to explain later. "The important thing now to be discussing is concrete and abstract aspiration, concrete and generalised action in many men and women of very many kinds of them and now there will be a beginning of discussing the feeling in each one of being a bad one, of being a good one, the relation of aspiration and action, of generalised and concrete aspiration and action" (538).

Aiming for concreteness, then, the narrator tells a story about a father who writes often to his daughter, Edith, about how she should not do anything to disgrace herself or him. He writes to her with this sentiment repeatedly, until one day the daughter "wrote back to tell him that he had not any right to write moral things in letters to her" (539). Her explanation is disturbing, suggesting incest and sounding very much like what we now call grooming:

> . . . that he had taught her that he had shown her that he had commenced in her the doing the things things that would disgrace her and he had said that when he had begun with her he had said he did it so that when she was older she could take care of herself with those who wished to make her do things that were wicked things and he would teach her and she would be
> (539) stronger than such girls who had not any way of knowing better . . .

After getting this letter, the father "was a paralytic always after," he was so shocked by it. He throws it in the fire and tells his wife over and over that Edith was trying to kill him. The mother asks if it was because Edith was disgracing them and he says no, but that she was killing him "and that was all he said then of the matter and he never wrote another letter" (539).

Setting aside the fact that Stein has her narrator revealing an all-too-common but unspoken patriarchal practice, this passage reinforces the revelation by continuing to examine it. "It happens very often," the narrator notes, and "This is very common," just as they noted about Martha's incident of unwanted contact from a boy. They add another incident of a father who convinces his son that it was cruel to collect butterflies and beetles, to kill things in order to have a collection. When the obedient son gives up collecting, the father gets up early and catches, kills, and pins "a wonderfully beautiful moth," heartlessly confusing the boy. But here's the thing: these men go on doing malicious things. "It happens very often that a man has it in him, that he does things, that he does something, that he does many things when he is a young man and an older man and an old man, that he feels always in a way about everything, that he is a good enough man in living, that he is a very good man." (540)

So, in the "very many kinds of men," among the "great many millions of them," there are always some who do "the concrete things" that are different from "the generalised feeling in them of what is right and decent and good and bad to be doing" (540). This emphasizes the theme of self-deception, but adds a nuance about how important this practice is to patriarchy, how "many kinds of men" do malicious things to women and children while believing all along that they are "very good" men. For seven allusive pages, the narrator considers and reconsiders this insight: "It happens very often that a man has it in him that he does something and that thing is a concrete acting and no one would ever think that man had done that thing and that man is a good man, and he does it very often" (541). To us, this seems straight from today's headlines, a century before it erupted into #metoo.

We want to point out, emphatically, that such revelations about commonplace violence were not ordinary at the time. This was a truth generally left unacknowledged, and one that Stein hides in the context of exploring "kinds of being," almost as if she were writing truths projected toward a later generation that could understand and accept them.[3]

We also want to note that the narrator twists this observation consistently with the other story, the "plot," linking it directly to the Dehning family—to Mr. Henry Dehning, to George Dehning, and even to Alfred Hersland, now associated with the family by marriage. Imagining oneself a good person while doing things that are "not of virtue in them" is a common thing, the narrator repeats. "[V]ery many men do it, very many men do it because they are in it, very many men do it for very many women, for some women, very many men do it for men and for women, and for other women,
(542 and for children, very many do it for very many, very many do it for some . . ."

543) And we go on, as the narrator again calls our attention to the process of writing about people and how difficult it is to realize "the whole of human being" (544). They remind us, again, of the goal to write "a complete description of all the kinds there are of men and women," but now noting that "sometime there will surely then be written" this description—not that *they* will write it; that is no longer the goal of this project we're reading. So, they say, let's get back to the specifics of the family we're dealing with here.

The narrator then begins to contemplate goodness, without, of course, returning to family as promised. "Being good then is a thing about which there will now be very much writing" (545). And they are as good as their word. As we puzzle over goodness, the text itself becomes visually striking in its repetition of the verbs that demonstrate the variety of people's "thinking, believing and feeling, always very often each one is thinking feeling believing something, sometimes they can afterwards be changing in that thinking, feeling, believing, knowing (545). This variety sometimes makes outliers difficult to understand, so they are accused of being "really

3. This fascinating idea of LGBTQIA authors optimistically writing forward for generations that will follow, generations whose sexuality won't be, of necessity, a well-guarded secret, is inspired by a presentation Cecilia heard at the first meeting of the Feminist Inter/Modernist Association in June 2018, Jodie Medd's "Modernism's Queer Temporal Resistance in the Space Between." Professor Medd, of Carleton University, explores this idea further in "Posthumous Queer Modernism" in the *Routledge Companion to Queer Theory and Modernism* (ed. Melanie Micir, forthcoming).

crazy" (546). But, truly, if anyone really knew what another person was "believing thinking knowing feeling doing" they would "be thinking that one a crazy one, would be afraid of such a one" (546). To the narrator, everyone is a little "crazy"; everyone is an outlier.

Reaching again for the concrete example, the text describes "a very intelligent active bright well-read fairly well-experienced woman" who is surprised to learn that women outside the circle of her religion, the Plymouth Brethren, have periods. She thinks that "what happens every month to all women" happened only and specifically to the women she knows intimately—until she learns otherwise when she is 28 years old (547). Other people are sure that no river can flow north because north, to them, is uphill. "Such things are very common" the narrator points out. You just never know what another person is "thinking feeling doing believing knowing" (547). And though the order of the verbs changes throughout, the repetition stands out on the page. The pattern continues as the narrator begins again with goodness, linking it to "religion and sensitiveness and feeling and loving, and realising and understanding and thinking and doing and knowing in every one, in every kind there is in men and women" (548). "It is very interesting" that people's beliefs often begin with loving someone enough to do what they do, or what they invite you to join them in doing.

Then suddenly the text breaks the pattern. "Dead is dead" (549). An unusual three-word sentence cuts through the narrative, and then "dead" leaps from the page in its frequency and in contrast to those rolling strings of the verbs of living:

> Dead is dead yes dead is really dead yes to be dead is to be really dead yes, to be dead is to be really dead and that is the real ending of them yes, but still, yes to be dead is to be dead, to be really dead yes, and yet always there is religion always existing and it is better to have everything, to be dead is to be dead some men are feeling knowing thinking believing in them, very many men are feeling thinking knowing believing it in them . . . dead is dead yes that is true then, and then they go on in living always doing their religion. (549)

Religion lets men believe that dead isn't dead, it "is always saying that though you are dead you are living," and with that we return to the men who do terrible things, who kill the moth or abuse the daughter. If dead is dead, there is no reason to resolve the conflict in self-perception that such acts inspire for "good" men, but if they are surrounded by religious people, those beliefs take hold and the men feel a need to "equilibrate themselves" (551). They develop "a generalised conviction" of their own virtue, "of having virtue in them when they are not doing any good thing of never doing anything any good man cannot be doing when really they are doing that thing very often . . ." (551).

We revisit this masculine self-deception, of "explaining ones vices by ones virtues" for several pages with a few more specific examples (551). One man justifies his mean behavior by blaming it on the awful person who inspires it. Another practices repeated infidelity, violating their commitment to one woman, so the next one, the new one "is to them the complete thing of idealistic romantic chastity for them" (554). Men like this have no need to hide their bad behavior, as religious men might do, "not be letting their right hand know what their left hand is doing" (552). Instead, they boast about how good they are. They are proud of themselves; "he is a good man completely a good one to himself inside him, that is all being in him, he is the complete thing of a generalised conviction of virtuous being" (553).

"It is very perplexing" in the end, that "many men and many women" can be so convinced of their own virtue while "acting that is not of virtue in them" (556). It is particularly perplexing for their families, "those knowing always the kind of them, this kind in men and women." So, the narrator notes, "Alfred Hersland will soon then be interesting" (556). But not yet. Returning to the contemplation of virtue, the text examines its sources—in religion or work or superstition or love. David Hersland, whose story is coming, is among those "who love themselves so much immortality can have no meaning for them" (557).

Another diversion reveals the narrator's strategy of writing things down before they understand them, so they can understand them: "This is pretty clear to my thinking, not completely clear yet and I am now telling it here

to a little rid myself of it to begin again to think and feel about it." Perhaps this (559)
contemplation is just preparing the way for what is to come, for the part of the story that will have to go back and forth from Alfred Hersland to Julia Dehning. "[A]nd so sometime perhaps everything will come to be showing something and that will be then a happy ending of all this beginning" (559). Because, we imagine, novels are expected to have happy endings; particularly, books authored by women are expected to have happy endings.

And now, 27 pages into this section, we seem to be ready for Alfred Hersland, who, through this exploration of violent masculinity, has become very clear to the narrator. They are "full up very full up now with a whole large group who are all more less connected in kind with him, with Alfred Hersland as he is completely now inside him, a complete one" (560). But wait. Let's first back up to Mr. Hissen, Alfred's grandfather, whose most important characteristics appear to be 1) that he is dead and 2) that he was religious. The concern with (and fear of) being "a dead one," with "knowing dead is dead" will continue from here through the rest of the novel (563). How people respond to this, whether they mark the inevitability of death or see "everything as never ending," helps to reveal their kind of being—and again we're reminded of resisting, loving, stubborn, attacking, independent dependent, religious feeling, virtuous feeling, "acting thinking being" as we seem to be coming nearer to a description of "Mr. Henry Dehning" (565).

Here the narrator circles back as they promise to move forward, checking in and summing up:

> There have been now, been in this description, the three generations of men and women. There was then Mr. and Mrs. Hissen and the old Mr. and Mrs. Hersland, there was then Mr. and Mrs. David Hersland and these then had three children Martha and Alfred and David and the history of Martha has been now already mostly written, not completely altogether written but a good deal written and now there will be beginning to be written the history of Alfred Hersland and every one he ever came to know in his early living, in his marrying and in his later living. (565)

The narrator touches on Alfred's family tree, particularly his ties to his grandfathers, but confesses: "I will be waiting and then I will be full up with all the being in him, that is certain, and so then now a little again once more then I am waiting waiting to be filled up full completely with him with all the being ever
(565) in him." While we're waiting, then, let's review. Certainly, he "was of the resisting kind of them," of the "dependent independent kind of them," of the "engulfing resisting kind in men and women" (566). As they revisit various types, the narrator comments charmingly on the process of waiting for clarity to arrive. Waiting is interesting in itself, they write, because "always something is coming or else nothing is coming," and, meanwhile, "there is eating, sleeping, laughing, living, talking and a little tickling in the body and the mind then that is very pleasant to anyone liking waiting" (567). It is clear that our narrator likes "very well doing waiting," because as they get "a little near to beginning," they continue to promise more to come on Alfred—and continue to defer that promise (567).

The development of Alfred's character begins to play a bigger part in the chapter now, though the narrative self-consciousness continues. We get a series of deferrals, page after page of shifts from "beginning waiting" for more clarity about Alfred while examining the painful process of writing. The seemingly troubled narrator now waits for Alfred to be "a whole one" even as "every one is in fragments inside me," and they despair of ever really knowing Alfred at any stage in his life (572). "Perhaps not any one really is a whole one inside them to themselves or to any one. Perhaps every one is in pieces inside them," they suggest (572). And this makes writing hard. When you write, "it is a very hard thing to be realising that some who would naturally be thinking the kind of way one writing is thinking are not ever thinking that kind of a way about anything, about something" (572). Authorial self-doubt creeps in and things fall apart.

"Every one to me just now is in pieces to me," the narrator reveals, as they are overcome by "a not very joyous feeling, having the emotion of having every one as a piece to one, it does not make of everything a thing without ending and all the time then there is not any use of anything keeping on going" (574). Like it or not, "this is now then the real state of feeling I am now having" (575). Here it becomes clear that the narrator is not pursuing a memoir, but a fiction. They describe how they invent characters by telling "about the living in them," but that's not enough; "from the living they have had in them I cannot ever construct action for them to be doing, I have certainly constructive imagination for being in them, sometimes with very little watching I have pretty complete realisation of pretty nearly all the being in them" (594). But then they return to real life models, arguing that they can only work from "the actual detail of the actual living of each actual one I am ever knowing" (594). At one point, these three sentences make up a stark paragraph about the writing process: "I am altogether a discouraged one. I am just now altogether a discouraged one. I am going on describing men and women." (605) Lost and discouraged, the narrator can only go on (like Beckett's *Unnamable*).

The authorial voice becomes increasingly and urgently self-conscious, letting us know the "Inside Baseball" of it all, such as how difficult it is to use a new word in their writing, because "Every word I am ever using in writing has for me very existing being" and all of its former existence is always present in each new use of the word (595). We move through the weight of this continuous present, from "This is now to be a description" (595), to a conjugal tour of verb tenses—"I will describe," "I am now describing," "I have been describing," repeatedly (595-620, throughout). And as we follow them along, the narrator fully becomes the story at hand, or at least (again) the most engaging character in it, as they strive to understand, to sort, to move toward wisdom:

> Some men and women are inquisitive about everything, they are always asking, if they see any one with anything they ask what is that thing, what is it you are carrying, what are you going to be doing with that thing, why have you that thing, where did you get that thing, how long will you have that thing, there are very many men and women who want to know about anything and everything, I am such a one, I certainly am such a one. (614)

The narrator here includes themself in the exploration of types, seeming to acknowledge our curiosity about them, even as they defer our curiosity back to the text. They point to their own questions, then use them to guide readers along, to pick up the fragments, gather disparate details about Alfred, and attend to many, many descriptions of "the kinds of being" in mostly unnamed men and women. They pause at one point, with a gasp of appreciation at how each one is "a lovely one to me" (608). They also affirm (in case your attention was flagging) that they are "certain they are right about everything" and when they are not right, "something is wrong" (632). At one point, we find ourselves in a rather pointed conversation as the narrator barks:

> I feel it and I brood over it and it comes then very simply from me, do you see how simply it comes out of me, you see, I feel it and I think about it and then I know it and I know then it is a simple thing, why are you always saying then it is a complicated one when really it is a very simple one this thing, do you see now it is a very simple thing this thing, do you see that this is a simple thing like everything why then should you make of it a complicated thing when it is a simple thing, do you see now that it is a simple thing this
> (622) thing, why do you make everything a complicated thing . . .

As the accusation continues, it becomes less apparent who is addressing whom, whether the narrator is personally engaging the reader or if they are describing other suspicious people, overly sensitive people or "very many people" who are "always saying this thing" (622). Point taken, though. We are clearly now entering the text by way of this powerful narrative voice that does not defer to Alfred or anyone. As we near the end of the next section break, the denouement comes first with the narrator, who finally, conclusively, identifies as a "dependent independent kind" with "quite a good deal always of dependent despairing," as if that's where we were heading all along. Of course; this section is about the narrator. They conclude, then, with another lament about *TMOA*: "I am going on writing, I am going on now with a description of all whom Alfred Hersland came to know in his living. Mostly no one will be wanting to listen. I am certain. I am
(656) important inside me and not any one really is listening." And we end with the promise to share more of the history of Alfred and Julia. OK.

*

From the beginning of this section (567-660) the narrator interlaces small strands of Alfred's life with the explanatory threads of their own insights. Doubling back, then, we pick up the mundane pieces of "Alfy's" boyhood in Gossols, examining one at a time the fragments of his place in the family, his musical ability, the people around him and those who share his type of being (the twos and fours and sixes, "a considerable number" of them). These fragments are mostly reiterations of what we have already seen about life in Gossols for the Hersland children, with a bit of perspective shift to the middle child. Apparently being the older son without being the oldest child is uncomfortable because "it is a nice thing, it is mostly pleasant for every one when the eldest son is the eldest of the children" (568). A quick review of the stages of his life—from babyhood to boyhood to college to marriage and beyond—is followed by what might constitute a physical description in this unusual development of character: "He was a good enough looking one, many said he was a very good looking one" (569).

Alfred, we learn, was even more connected than Martha was with "the country people" in small houses around him, where "no other rich people lived" (582). He roller skated, camped, fished, played hide and seek, and "did with the girls everything a boy does when he is with them" (586). We get a cataloguing of his friends—the three Banks boys, Louis Champion, Frank and Will Roddy, the four Fisher children, and the four Henrys. We find that Alfred "was neither popular nor very unpopular with those who knew him" (592). He was "a good citizen" and claimed his place as the older son, presiding over Martha, who was three years older, and threatening her with exposure to their father when she was out in the evenings—because their father permitted him an independence she wasn't afforded. We learn he had musical ability, that he played the violin and that he had a music teacher named Mr. Arragon.

The effort to write about Alfred, as we described above, seems often to be beyond the narrator, as when they interrupt to declare: "**Alfred Hersland was of a kind of men and women. This is now some description of that kind of them.**" Thirty-five pages of explorations of type follow that brief (597)
paragraph, with only occasional mention of Alfred. It seems there is just not enough Alfred to make a full character, so we get to know him as

"the engulfing resisting being," "active and aspiring" and, like others of his type, "very completely live ones in their existing" (598-9), even as the narrator tries repeatedly to pull the pieces of his life together. They hold onto every small bit because they are shoring details up, like milk that should not be wasted: "Such a one can have it that that one never throws away anything, never wastes anything in living, and always there is more milk there than one can be using in the daily living" (599). All well and good, because this exploration of types offers the opportunity for funny details, like the return of "lying, stupid being" (601), or the man who has "in him very thickly in him murky resisting engulfing being," or (our favorite of this group) the description of a person "like a cannon-ball lying on a bag of cotton" (620). Even better is the doubt that follows: "This is not a funny description, I was not certain I should say anything of the cannon-ball
(621) and the cotton."

To know Alfred, though, the narrator promises to send us to "the man who was a musician" and "the woman who was the sister of the first governess," because these two "were a little important" to him "in his early living as I have already been saying" (636). But beginning with the musician, Mr. Arragon, leads away again, to a discussion of the distinctions between passion and affection. Arragon was passionate, but not poignantly so, except to other people who saw the "weakness and sensitiveness and romance in him" (639). As the narrator spins away from Alfred and Arragon, in a further cataloguing of types, they mention Martha Hersland as "Martha Redfern" or "Mrs. Redfern," and place her among the "passionate creating seizing attacking kind in men and women" (639). But back to Arragon, who mattered to Alfred because "Alfred Hersland really had musical feeling and musical understanding in him"; Alfred "was very much with" Arragon, who was "as important as anyone to Alfred Hersland then" (645). There's a brief mention of a schoolteacher (a sister of the governess, Ida) who both Alfred and Arragon liked, but it turned out that she "was a queer one to mostly every one knowing her" (649). She was also "a stupid resisting, stagnant, dull fairly sensible one" with a "nervous kind of crazy kind of asking every one to be a lover to her" (651).

And that's about as far as we get with young Alfred (or Arragon or

Ida) before we return to the narrator's frustration with trying to depict this central character who seems so unaffected by everyone around him "in his early living." Leaving Gossols behind, the narrator adds more detail after Alfred arrives in Bridgeport for school. He makes a good impression on the Hissen relatives there, who connect with him because "though he was a fairly tall one he looked a little like them and was very pleasant in liking them" (652). Later we get this delightful description: **"In the beginning living he was interesting to some as realising musical meaning, and mostly then he was pleasantly young and quite tall and always giving romantically scientifically restrained superior information and playing the violin not very well but always able then to be directing the one playing with him."** Eventually Alfred gets tired (655)
of the familial attention (and the violin). Meanwhile, the Hissens could apparently tear a woman down if Alfred showed any interest in her. Led by one interfering aunt, Hilda, they "helped Alfred to not want then to be marrying," when he had been in school for only two years and wanted to quit and go into business. It worked. That particular girl moved away and wrote some letters that everyone made fun of, and Alfred kept studying. Three years later (653) or a year and a half later (654), he is involved with Julia Dehning, the first woman who made him "very seriously feeling loving" (654). And now, the narrator promises, we will learn more about Julia, who "was of the attacking kind in men and women," of her history, of those who knew her "and of every thing" (658).

Pages 660–793 | Alfred and Julia marry in this section. It may seem as though they married multiple times over, but we promise it's just the once. Oh, and "[t]hey were not successful together in their married living" (664). But you knew that was coming.

We begin on a freshly indented page with anecdotes about living pleasantly. There are various ways to live pleasantly or unpleasantly, and Alfred Hersland, without a doubt, lives pleasantly in his early days in Bridgeport. "Later then living was exciting and interesting and gay and varied and absorbing and perplexing and sometimes disconcerting and sometimes uneasy in him but it was never again I am thinking so pleasant in him" (660). So, we return to that early time when Alfred is going back and forth about the girl who went away, trying to decide whether or not to spend his life with her (661). In his "beginning living," Alfred cannot possibly predict his own potential successes and failures, a common struggle for everyone according to the narrator, because "very many are not knowing what is in them to really come out of them" (661). But, listen, they remind us: to understand what they are capable of, human beings must develop an understanding of their own repeating. Repeating, it might surprise you to know, is the key. And yet many will never see this unless they are willing to acknowledge their "being always repeating" in the first place (662).

The narrator reaffirms their love for repeating, and reminds us how unique it makes them because "mostly every one is telling that they do not love repeating, they do not think it at all a lovely thing" (663). Not our narrator, who asserts their singularity: **"And here I am almost all alone in really completely loving repeating, loving it that each one all his living is**
(663) **repeating all his being."** Refusing to learn from our own repeating behaviors is a monumental reason why "very many as I was saying are not learning about themselves in living" (663). Acknowledging our own repetitions, then, our narrator reaffirms, is essential to self-understanding.

Loving becomes the topic at hand, then, as we circle around it, dip into it, then draw back and survey it for the next several pages. "There are very many degrees of having loving in men and women" (664), and many ways that loving is expressed "sometimes concentrated, sometimes very diffused in them, sometimes in lumps in them" (666). Our narrator notes that many people have qualms with the various ways others display "loving feeling": "A very great many have very many prejudices concerning loving," they point out, "more perhaps even than about drinking and eating. This is very common. Not very many are very well pleased with other people's ways of having loving in them" (667). But the narrator does not hold such prejudices. **"I like loving. I like mostly all the ways any one can have of having**
(669) **loving feeling in them."**

With the now familiar deferred promise of soon beginning to home in on Julia and Alfred, the narrator veers toward another metafictional detour, telling us how difficult it is to do the work they do, observing people and revealing their character, how miserable and sometimes hopeless this task makes them. They have seen so many people lately, and the more people they see the more their frustration grows with distinguishing what type and kind category each person belongs to. It is a complex task, and "I am wearied with seeing and not seeing being in them," they tell us. "[W]earied and not wearied with my learning," they are still happy, they insist. "I am a happy one, that is quite reasonably certain. I am quite a very happy person. I am quite completely a very happy person seeing very many men and women." Surprisingly, the narrator seems hesitant to begin unfolding (671) Julia's character for us. Julia is an attacking kind of person, and the narrator wants to be honest about that. "I am beginning preparing myself now to be courageous to do this thing" (672).

But first another dive into to the narrator's misery, depression, and jealousy, their "sad and sombre feeling," their certainty that they "would be always being nearer and more nearly a completely dead one" (672). The narrator ponders "the feeling of dreaming" they get when examining the type of being in friends, family, or new acquaintances. As the dream breaks, we wake up and realize the type of being we thought existed within somebody was only our imagination (673). Through these pages, we see the narrator taking on the now familiar task of trying to become "full up" with a character, in this case Julia, before writing about them. And as they work toward that point, they review what they know, say it differently, repeat and repeat what they see, associate the character at hand with others like them, see them from another angle, try out another verb tense or simply defer. And they ruminate on how it feels to be searching for their character's essence, their "being," on how it feels to see and to write. "I am a little melancholy with it in me now," they write (674). "I am enjoying"; "I get an awful sinking feeling"; "I am desolate"; "I am almost sulking"; "I am saying"; "I am loving repeating"; "I am tired"; and, finally, "I am realising Alfred Hersland and Julia Dehning" (674-75).

Here the narrator reaches back to the Dehning family in what they assure us will be a comparison. What follows is a brief (-ish) reflection on the fathers of the two families, Henry and David. They begin on the predicted path with the story of Mr. Henry Dehning ("a foreign american"), contrasting his self-made success as an immigrant with Mr. David Hersland's failure to achieve the "rich right american living" (676). Another stark contrast to David Hersland's temper, lack of empathy and understanding towards his children is Dehning's generous and kind nature toward his family. Dehning's wife, Jenny, does not believe he can function without her, and regrets that she dies before him. "She was the first one to be a dead one as I am saying" (677); "she was a little lonesome one in dying, she was knowing that her husband who was a very good man and a very devoted one would be needing a woman to fill him, she knew his children should not want for their sake that he should marry some one" (678).

The relationship between Jenny and Henry is built on mutual adoration and respect in a way that we do not see with the Herslands, David Sr. and Fanny, because of David's intolerance and his belief that he alone should reign supreme over the household. We learn over and over that Jenny maintains a lot of control over her husband, and she uses it whenever she pleases. The narrator describes Henry as gentle, warm, not stupid, always ready, and even a bit of a pushover; whereas Jenny is filled with attacking being but is not unpleasant (681).

Through all of this, the narrator is "almost ready to feel all being there is or was or will be in Julia Dehning," returning, revealingly, to the idea of courage. Those who possess it have an easier time doing "ordinary living," they tell us. "**For some it takes courage to be killing anything, like a buzzing thing or a fly, to buy anything, to sell anything, to eat anything, to drink anything, to**
(677- **want anything, to forget anything, to decide anything, to like anything.**" And,
678) too, it takes courage to face the task of writing about Julia. We feel the narrator gathering that courage—and, again, reviewing, deferring and repeating, as they do.

We leave the Herslands behind, then, and return to the Dehnings, reiterating that Henry Dehning, like Jenny Dehning, was not unpleasant but neither was he "a pleasant one" (680). They lived "the right very rich american living" and both felt their own independent importance inside of themselves (680). Mrs. Dehning, it turns out, was "in a way a gay one" and "in a way a stupid one," and "had a sense for living, that was certain" (681). Astonishingly, the narrator also reveals that both Dehnings are "whole ones" to them, which we readers know is not an easy state of being to achieve. "Mrs. Dehning was a whole being" (681). "Mr. Dehning was a whole one in living" (682). After a few breaks to catch us up on the narrator's progress ("I like to hear everything"; "I like to know the living in every one"; " I am loving to be knowing"; "I am learning"; "I am haltingly learning"; "I am realising"), they inform us that "sometime I will know what I am now doing" in trying to identify kinds of each and every one that is or ever will be living (683-85). And we're back to embracing that challenge again, approaching it now through the Dehning family's "fairly free very rich very decent right american living" (688); "The Dehnings then were then living, very pleasantly, quite entirely decently, not very aggressively, pretty freely, quite contentedly, fairly advancedly, thoroughly generously, quite gayly, pretty entirely cheerfully, right very rich american living" (686).

A lovely long paragraph follows, consisting mostly of one sentence full of phrases in progressive present tense, making a striking pattern on the page. It sets up with "Mostly every one has living has some kind of meaning to them" (688) then launches into "living, working, loving, dressing, dreaming, walking" then adding participles such as "being one liking eating, being one liking thinking, being one liking waking, being one certainly not afraid to be dying" and on and on from -ing to -ing (688-90). The paragraph concludes with a series of shorter fragments centering on the narrator who pleads (as we might be doing):

> There are all these ways then of having living having meaning and there are innumerable other ones, do not crowd so on me the other ones, I know very well there are very many other ones, I know very well I am not knowing all the ways men and women are feeling living, I know very well I am not knowing all the ways one can have living have meaning. (689)

Then we begin (again) to catalog information about Julia, approaching the larger, daunting task of understanding all men and women by way of a careful specific case. She liked her children; she had "attacking being" and "was to mostly every one a completely honest one"; she was "an excited and ambitious one"; she was nervous and "was a stupid one"; she "had not really sense for living"; "she had real courage in her, that is certain" (690-95). These few pages are a fine example of how the novel inventories multiplies types of traits as they intersect in a single character's being.

We learn, as this cataloguing continues, that the narrator is getting there, getting to certainty about Julia. "I know Julia Dehning" a paragraph begins" (695). Certainly, yes of course, I know, have known, will know, have come to know, Julia Dehning, repeats in some form nearly twenty times in the space of one page, and concludes, "**I am certainly certain I am certainly**
(696) **knowing being in Julia Dehning.**" Yet the cataloguing and the repetition go on, as we think about the sensitivity, the ability to learn, and nervousness in Julia and other women. Then the narrator turns back, ready to begin again, "to commence my regular description of being in Julia Dehning, of Dehning family living, of Julia's meeting and marrying of loving and not learning, and not enduring Alfred Hersland, and of her complete living. I am beginning again, not from the beginning this time, that is certain" (703).

The focus shifts, then, to "family living," and how the Dehning family's life is not something that can be understood from the outside looking in. Each family varies in their type of family living, a living made up of the beings of family members colliding, creating something distinctive to them: "It certainly is quite entirely a difficult thing to keep on a long time with several living in a house together, a family to go on really listening to what each one is telling, to what each one is needing, having for living" (704). The Dehning family's harmonious existence is not without the usual hardships that exist between family members, but the real contrast between the Dehnings and Herslands is in the gap between their levels of harmony.

We revisit the birth order of the Dehning children—Julia, George, and Hortense—reiterating information from the very earliest pages of the novel, and then we return to plumbing the depths of Julia's character. Some aspects of Julia's personality seem difficult for the narrator to access, so they reveal other, banal things about her—that she lacks a sense of self-awareness or personal responsibility, for example. A woman of her time, Julia expects to maintain a relationship with a man who will provide for her financially. Because she doesn't need to handle this herself, Julia decides that she can't be touched by failure; there will always be somebody around to support and take care of her. This perception acts as a double bind for a privileged white woman, where she can't develop personal independence because of the strictures of her society, but, at the same time, she is condemned for her lack of independence, for her submission to the life she has been forced to accept as the correct version of a fairytale.

We learn that Julia's mother lives with a similar quandary. She is nervous, and her sense of nervousness comes (like Mrs. Hersland's) from her children not needing her anymore. Neither Jenny nor Julia have any real desire for success beyond incorporating "Dehning family traditions" into their lives and family living. "Julia had not the emotion of ambition," but the family "was living a successful, generous, pleasant, reasonably important very rich american living" (706, 707). So, Julia was successful, in her way, and we're reminded that Alfred and Julia, in their early days, at the beginning of the novel, "did certainly have loving in them each one of them for the other one" (707). Alfred drops everything to marry Julia because her love is, at one point, all he wants. But that changes over time.

An intriguing few passages about identity then interrupt the narrative about **"Julia and Alfred and Dehning family living and loving and learning and quarrelling."** The narrator reflects on how some people know themselves (710)
and demonstrate this in their ways of living and dressing and in "what they are wanting from every one, from any one" (710). Some know who they are but don't show it or can only show it with some people, or can't remember it when they're alone. "Some know what they want to be and can build it by little pieces and do again and again." Some are constantly inventing themselves. Poignantly, some hold back, hiding who they are: "Some see what they want to be in daily living and in dressing and then they are a little less than that thing so that they will not be queer to any one" (710). A dressmaking metaphor guides through this passage, with cutting and fitting and finishing linked to Julia's ways of living.

Then we're back to processing what we know about Julia, remembering, realizing, repeating who she is, exploring the intersections of her types of

being—attacking, winning, generous, loving, resisting and stupid. "Julia Dehning was quite an important person in being a person being living" (713). When we begin to read how she comes to be with Alfred, things get tense. This is no surprise, given that some form of this sentence has reappeared every time they are mentioned: "They were married then and they did not succeed in their married living together then" (715). But now the narrative fills in some details only hinted at earlier, beginning with this brief paragraph: **"Mr. Dehning soon came to thinking that Alfred Hersland was not an honest man. Julia Hersland soon came to be certain that Alfred Hersland was not an honest one. Mr. Dehning was an honest enough man in living. That**
(716) **is certain."**

While all of them "had some loving feeling in them"—Mr. and Mrs. Dehning, Julia and Alfred—Alfred's attempt to use his connection to Julia's father to help him achieve success (he had then "important feeling for being one aspiring to succeeding in living") is thwarted when Mr. Dehning discovers his son-in-law's double dealing (717). Apparently, honesty is a Dehning family value, so Henry's impeccably honest nature helps him to identify Alfred's dishonesty.

We should point out that all through this portion of the story—the vaguely plot-driven romance novel portion—the narrator still pushes plot aside and takes center stage fairly regularly, asserting what they are "beginning to feel," what they know or are coming to know, what they see and what they are saying. This leads to a monologue that suggests that they can't really figure out *why* Alfred and Julia just didn't work together. **"I see some kinds of men and women, I look long at some of these kinds in men and women and I see nothing of the way they do their loving. And then I am very much**
(726) **regretting I do not yet know everything."**

What to do but what they always do: the narrator circles back and reconsiders, revisiting the early days of the Hersland/Dehning marriage. After the couple marries, Jenny comes "to have feeling for married living in Mr. and Mrs. Alfred Hersland. She could then fondle him some, Alfred Hersland, and make of him a son-in-law in Dehning family living" (727). The vivid picture of Mrs. Dehning putting her hands on Alfred to, in a metaphorical sense, change him into somebody worthy of being a son-in-law to the "right rich" Dehning parents comes across loud and clear. What is unclear is how much individuality the Dehnings will allow in their family circle.

Unlike his wife, Henry quickly loses faith in Alfred, even as Jenny continues to believe the couple is doing fine. Hortense and George even have opinions, although they are too young to judge, and that is enough about them. **"To go on then."** (729)

The narrator reminds us that some people believe they don't need to learn anything, which is specifically relevant here because Julia is obviously overlooking something. "This then is a description of Julia Hersland having been just then a married one" (728). Julia, normally excited to learn, is blindly disregarding what she would generally, shrewdly, see. Because she is "a married one," Julia misses obvious signs that Alfred is acting shady.

Alfred's unhappiness, his "needing something to make him completely be then one being really living" and "his coming not to be having, to be having this thing" goes to his father-in-law for help (729). Henry Dehning has his own idea of what success should look like, but he listens to Alfred and is eventually "convinced by Alfred Hersland's telling what Alfred Hersland was needing for succeeding in living" (730). This personality trait, this openness and love of conversation, you may recall, is something Mr. Dehning demonstrates early in the novel in his conversations with Julia. The narrator notes and expands on this generous parenting. And abruptly, the narrator intervenes again to focus on the process of writing and what they are learning through it. It's so delightful to them that they interrupt Alfred's story to let us know that **"I like it that I am feeling that I could be a very happy one if every one were certain I was a completely wise one."** (732)

At some point in Alfred's new life as a Dehning son-in-law, then, he receives "a good deal of money" as a loan from Mr. Dehning (732). But things start to go wrong, because Alfred "was not ever really succeeding in living" (733). As the novel begins to divulge Alfred's failure, the narrator seems to resist moving forward with the story, as if they don't want to face what's ahead: **"Now I am going on. Now go on."** Amid reflections on success (733)
and failure, beginning and ending, quarrelling, learning and wisdom, the narrator does move slowly forward with the story of Alfred: "Mr. Dehning

was helping Alfred Hersland as Alfred Hersland had wanted Mr. Dehning to help him. I was saying that Mr. Dehning came to help Alfred Hersland in the way Alfred Hersland had been wanting Mr. Dehning to help him. I told something about this thing" (735). But soon everyone was quarrelling—"Mr. Dehning and Julia Hersland and Mrs. Dehning then came to be quarrelling with Alfred Hersland" (735). Henry publicly reveals Alfred's character, how he "was not honest enough for daily living" (736). Then Alfred's reputation among those connected to his father-in-law deteriorates. The person who really needs convincing, though, is Julia, even though she is aware soon after marrying him that "Alfred Hersland was not an honest one in living an honest one for living" (739). It takes her a while to admit the truth, but, at last, it is undeniable. The rose-colored glasses come off. We revisit this evolution over the next several pages, how both Henry and Julia slowly come to be convinced of Alfred's dishonesty.

But first we take one more look at their marriage. "The Herslands Alfred and Julia were living married living. They had a baby and it was quite a strong well one but it did not live to be a very old one. It got sick and died of something" (740). This sad and glossed over declaration about the little boy who looked like his father is followed by a brief description of Julia's surviving children, a girl who looks like her mother and a third child, another boy, who is weak, but eventually grows stronger. Mr. Dehning is convinced that this boy is "a good deal like the father of him," but, thankfully, he is also a little like his "young uncle George Dehning" (740). The couple eventually decides to split, unable to overcome their differences, despite having children together. After some unspecified amount of time passes, they each "came to love another" (740). And then we conclude their story: "Sometime then they went on being living in married living with each other and then they were not and then they had more living in them and then one and then the other one was ended in being living" (741).

Segueing from the demise of this couple, the narrator moves to confronting "ending being in all men and in all women." Revisiting one of the novel's earliest themes, they encounter their own mortality, their "young being having been":

> I am feeling again and again in myself going to be an old one. I do not like this thing, I certainly do like this thing. I certainly do like ending being in all men and in women. I certainly do not at all like this thing. I certainly have completely a queer disturbed mixed with sombre feeling in this thing. I certainly do really completely need feeling certainly this thing in every one that each is sometime ending in being living. (741)

And they go on. They reflect on their desire to know all kinds of men and women, even while they continue to resist, and embrace, the idea that everyone's "being living" eventually ends. They discuss success and how it seems to clear the mind in a negative way, how it blinds the person experiencing it from "having a normal sense for living (744). And then "sense for living" takes over for several pages, followed by a return to types of being, to "this one" and "that one" and how people vary in their being—in size and shape as well as in attitude and measures of success. At one point, "there are eight of them" who may or may not be family members of Julia and Alfred, and who vary in their "sense for living," in their completeness, whether they are married or living or dead. We suspect that our job is not to know for certain who these people are, to distinguish their individuality or type, but to absorb the narrator's wisdom about humanity in general.

The narrator's verbs in this section slide away from certainty toward "I am wondering" and "I am thinking" (755). They are feeling, learning, realising, enjoying, not forgetting, and moving toward this conclusion: "I (756)
am then one in a way certainly one knowing everything." Thus, we have (certainly now but soon to be qualified) arrived.

We loop back once again to review the marriage that has dominated this section. With another spin on the traditional happily-ever-after, the narrator notes that Julia's initial pleasure in being married to Alfred didn't last long. "She liked it a little then and then it went on to come to be quite soon a beginning of a long ending, a long dividing of themselves from living with each other any more in being in living." We get the added detail that, though it (758)
took her longer than her husband, "Mrs. Dehning was certain then that Julia never should have been allowed to be married to him and this was

in her then a very certain thing" (759). It was finally unanimous. Jenny, too, comes solidly around to the family's negative assessment of Alfred.

The narrator promises to "go on with him, then I will go on with her," revealing that Alfred Hersland later marries Minnie Mason, but later in his life "he had had, did have, would have loving feeling for Julia Hersland and her children" (761). (*Editorial Note: Aren't they his children too? C'mon Alfy!*) At one point, his own brother, David, wonders if Alfred truly loves anyone. And then he's dead again: "So then Alfred lived and went on living and ended one having in him not enough sense for living to be one failing, to be one succeeding in living" (762). While he was married twice and worked well with some men, he was "pretty nearly a completely hated one in Dehning family living and being then a tradition as a hated one not honest in daily living in Dehning family living" (762). Then Julia dies, and the narrator is done here: "I am not finding it very interesting knowing what was happening later to the children of Alfred and Julia Hersland" (762).

But wait. There's a bit more to tell about Alfred, who, after he left Julia and "her children" (who he "sometimes for a little time saw one of them"), is "very nearly succeeding" in his living. He has friends like the successful Pat Moore who helps him out when he is finally ready to admit that he isn't the best at everything (763). Alfred relinquishes his hold over some things that he can't control, then meets Minnie Mason through his friends James Flint, the clothing manufacturer, and Mackinly Young, the musician and avid learner (764). Minnie, it turns out, is good at being married, having done it twice and having been in love three times. Here we learn a bit about Alfred's post-Julia friends who, the narrator informs us, respect and admire each other very much.

A few pages in the narrator interrupts these details about Alfred as they confront, again, their own mortality, this time with an added self-congratulation for recognizing it, for being certain of it. "I like living
but I am certain that I cannot know everything and so I know certainly that I will
be one some day not being any longer living. This is not to me a sorrowful thing,
this is to me now quite a certain thing. I like being living, I like too being certain
(767) of something."

After spending some time with Minnie and her contented married living with Alfred, the narrator allows that they know more than they are telling, with a shift to "as I could be saying" (773). A discussion ensues regarding "loving" and how it has the power to be a nice thing to some, and a not nice thing to others (774). Although Alfred remarries, Julia never does, as the man she might have married, William Beckling, becomes sick and refuses to marry her, because it wouldn't be fair to burden Julia with a chronically ill spouse. But Julia, too, has a long list of friends, which the narrator catalogues, complete with irrelevant names and vague time periods (777). What follows for a few pages is an analysis of the success level of those friends and how they intersect with Julia. William, for example, was "brilliantly succeeding in living" before he "came to be a sick one" (780).

The narrator then catches us up on their own progress, how they are finally achieving wisdom about the kinds of being in men and women, mostly by way of writing this book, "so then I will go on writing, and not for myself and not for any other one but because it is a thing I certainly can be earnestly doing with sometimes excited feeling and sometimes happy feeling and sometimes longing feeling and sometimes almost indifferent feeling and always with a little dubious feeling" (781). Note the shift here from writing "for myself and others" to writing because I can't stop myself. And so they go on: **"I could though be so wise and am so wise and it would be so nice for me to be certain that from me some other one could be a wise one a little less wise than I am who am the original wise one."** Let's savor (781)
that for a moment and repeat: "I am almost certain I am completely a wise one" (781). We all want to see that quote on a Stein stein.

In fact, we live for these metafictional moments, the revelations of a witty, word-loving narrator/writer who is, yet is not, Stein herself. As they charge toward the end of this section obsessing now about "dead ones," they insert: "I was telling some one yesterday evening, no I do not think I was telling any one this thing yesterday evening" (783). That's a sentence. It stands out for being unusually short, but it is also amusing in its pretension of intimacy and casual conversation. It underlines that this whole writing business is pretension—but that it is also serious and revealing. "I cannot come to be more certain ever of anything than I am of how very interesting it is to me in my being one being living to be certain of the feeling there is being in each one and how that feeling comes out of each one as expression." Knowing people has been the pursuit all along, and finding them in their expressions, in their repetitions, being, as the narrator is, "one loving hearing seeing feeling repeating has made of me a very wise one" (784). This is followed by a string of thoughts on "having a completely queer feeling," consistently a suggestive word play in this text (784).

The section concludes with Julia as a dead one, and a prolonged discussion of dead ones—relatives, friends and strangers. We are introduced to the inevitable possibility of the Dehning family dying out. With a final hurrah, the narrator tells us that they know a good deal about people of all ages at this point, because they have lived through each age with their main characters, "now" all in their sixties (788). Julia's important life events are summarized again, and the people she encounters are listed and listed again. And we end this section with the insight that we all have a difficult time discovering our own being, yet it's possible to do so, particularly through other people. We can go on with an awareness of "being in living" if we pay attention. The final paragraph, repetitive and rhythmic, difficult to make sense of with traditional reading practices, sets the tone for the remainder of the novel.

Part Three

[DAVID HERSLAND]

Pages 797–904 | In its entirety, the David Hersland section is less about telling a cohesive story and more about layering sentences on top of one another with simple, complementary words. The following is, we're sure, difficult to believe—but there is less plot here than anywhere else in the novel. The trajectory of the novel has been, for the most part, away from plot and into form, sound, and experimentation with words. If, to this point, most readers (like us) have held onto the threads of a story, we are about to be schooled away from that reading mode.

The now-familiar narrator reappears with the same concerns and similar phrasings here at the beginning of the David section. David, it seems, is a kindred spirit, who "liked thinking about feeling such things, thinking such things being in men and women," things like "that about which I have just been telling," the narrator notes (797). But not when he was younger, only "in his later living." And the inevitable promise follows: "This is to be now a history of him." But, of course, it isn't. Not a biography or history, a story or a novel in any traditional sense, this section is most characteristic of the enigmatic and playful style Stein later became famous for.

In the David section, the narrator deploys words to various purposes, to the extent that the chosen words lose their meaning or end up contradicting themselves, corresponding with many of Stein's explorations of the arbitrariness of language (as in "a rose is a rose is a rose"). Discussing David (and then nobody in particular) in meandering passages, the narrator refers to people as "this one" or "that one" or even groups of people, as "some."

Thus, we offer this hint: A helpful way to think about David's section—when it (frustratingly) veers off into multiple personalities (or "ones")—is to imagine that each sentence about a character is significant in how it works to form, layer by layer, the entire being of a complete person. We know from earlier in the novel that this wholeness can't be achieved until, if ever, the narrator's repetitions fill them up and a character's being takes shape. So, as we work through the repetitions, we wait, with the narrator, to be "full up" with them.

The first few pages revisit "being in living" and dead ones, certainty and the continuous present—"I do ask"; "I am believing"; "I certainly am not knowing" (797-98). The narrator speculates about what people do and don't do for one another. "Perhaps one is certain about that one about this thing. I know I am not certain about what I would do for some one, what I would not do for some one" (798). Certainty is a big topic of discussion throughout David's section, yet the more the narrator discusses certainty, the less confident they become. We learn that David Hersland didn't live to be old, that he "was dead before he came to the middle of his middle living" (799). Beginning his story with his death, shifting between certainty and self-doubt, the narrator leads with grief, lamenting that "no one will listen while I am talking" (801). And here's an interesting detail: "Some will listen while they are fat ones, they do not listen when after dieting they
(801) have become thin ones." Some young people listen "now very often" (801).

But, oh my God, what *can* the narrator do with their inability to experience and describe the different ways of being in living? See for yourself:

> I am in desolation and my eyes are large with needing weeping and I have a flush from feverish feeling and I am not knowing what way each one is experiencing in being living and about some I am knowing in a general way and I could be knowing in a more complete way if I could be living more with

> that one and I never will live more with every one, I certainly cannot ever live with each one in their being one being living, in my being one being living. (803)

This moment of despair seems to push the narrator to retreat, to engage with the novel differently. Once this paragraph full of I-statements ends, the narrator, as the metafictional, self-reflective character we have gotten used to, slowly disappears. Even the recurrences of "As I was saying" or "As I am saying" are few and far between. The paragraphs in this section focus on David or other "ones": "He was . . ."; "David Hersland was . . ."; "Each one . . ."; "There are . . ."; so when we arrive at another paragraph of self-revelation nearly 50 pages later, it stands out.

Here, in one sentence, the narrator seems to lose faith in words altogether:

> I mean, I mean and this is not what I mean, I mean that not any one is saying what they are meaning, I mean that I am feeling something, I mean that I mean something and I mean that not any one is thinking, is feeling, is saying, is certain of that thing, I mean that not any one can be saying, thinking, feeling, not any one can be certain of that thing, I mean I am not certain of that thing, I am not ever saying, thinking, feeling, being certain of this thing, I mean, I mean, I know what I mean. (862-3)

And with this, we suspect that the narrator is finally realizing how to be "full up" with a character, perhaps finally melding with David, their concerns becoming one for the rest of the section, leaving little room for an "I." Here, to understand a character, or another person, is to realize how little you can understand, even if you try, even if you believe in the possibility of understanding. The only certainty you end with is in your lack of certainty. Amid the repetitions and wanderings of this section, the thread of information about David unravels slowly even as the narrator disappears. Even so, we end up feeling that we know David better than any other character the narrator has introduced.

But before we arrive at this moment of recognition, we will turn back to earlier in the chapter, to the original spoiler, when David dies without ever becoming "an old one" (799). Our still-present narrator skips over the details of his death in favor of the mundane aspects of his life. After he is gone, many people wonder if David would have been successful had he lived, but there is irony in even asking this question, because asking can't lead to any answers. Revisiting David's death seems both comfortable and completely disturbing for the narrator, who expresses understanding and compassion, letting readers know that they too, find it unnerving when somebody is suddenly or inexplicably claimed by death. Anecdotes follow about how some people are completely satisfied with their lives when it is time for them to die, whereas some are not ready and fear dying. Whether people have a more difficult time accepting the death of a young person versus an older person occupies the narrator; they wonder if having lived more life is reason for death to be less distressing.

Some older preoccupations return here as well. The narrator points out that the stages of our lives so dominate our thinking that it's hard to imagine the stage beyond where we are, how to think about being an old one when we are young or in our middle living. "Listening doesn't help with this thing," they point out, because of "the difficulty each one has of realising whole being" (806-7). Even when older folks talk about being younger, "it is a description of an old one having been a young one, not a realising of being a young one, and so on and so on" (807).

We are also led through more details about types of being, with the narrator describing conversations with unnamed people. These unnamed people represent different *types* of inner being (keep in mind these are types, not kinds). "[B]ut as I was saying each one of a kind in men and women has being in that one being differently in him from being in any other one of that kind of them (805). An important distinction is made here. Many people can belong to a category of a "kind," but a "type of being" has no limit. Within a category of a kind of personality, there can be people with an infinite number of differences in being. It's possible that here in the narrator's quest to uncover all types of people that will ever be living, they are (finally) suggesting that the task was insurmountably large for one determined narrator to accomplish, and "kinds" becomes another overarching way to categorize other personality traits. Repetitions quantify qualities and kinds throughout this section, such as the amount of "talking or listening" each "one" does. The verbs vary throughout, from talking and listening to feeling and smelling.

And here we include another reading hint. Something to keep in mind throughout this section is the way the verb tenses repetitively shift. It helped us to try to keep track of the differences that these tense shifts made in our reading. When the sentences are so utterly thick with repetitive vagueness, it helps to have something else to keep an eye out for, so a change from past to present can help. **"I am thinking then about telling about knowing being being in men and in women. I am thinking them about listening and talking being, going to be being, having been being in some men in some women."** (808) Here, the narrator is thinking right now, with us in this moment, but in some instances throughout David's section they use the phrase "I have been thinking," suggesting a different time frame. We are now, of course, familiar with the ever repeating "As I was saying," and because it appears less often we become more aware of it when it does appear. Later, it comes as almost a shock to read "As I *am* saying" (858, 860) [emphasis added].

But back to David, who is, like the narrator, interested in really *living*, in being full up with life. Anything David can learn he wants to know, and anything he can do he wants to try—again, like the narrator, who, you may recall, declared they are "such a one" who is incurably curious (614). David is engaged in the present, lives in the present, and listens avidly to those around him. "He was one mostly all his living almost completely interested in his being one going on being living" (809). It is repeated that he was born in Gossols where he experienced half country-half city living, but we also learn that he was born to parents who really wanted three children but, after Martha and Alfred, had lost two. He understood from "quite a young one" that "being living is a very queer thing, he being living and yet it was only because two others had not been ones going on living" (819). We see that the experiences of childhood and how he came to "being living" remain influential throughout David's life. He was "wanting it that he should be one realising every minute what there was in life" (821).

In living every minute, he also wants to be a loving person, to know and to love women: "He would have liked all of his living to feel beauty in any kind there is of women . . . He certainly would have liked very well all his living to be finding every woman every kind of woman a beautiful one in being loving" (811). Yet, it appears that regardless of what he wants, David can't seem to find women collectively attractive. He never marries, though he knows someone, "this one," very well (828). On the other hand, the narrator repeats that women love in many different ways, and that women who feel important inside have a knack for making David Hersland completely submissive to them (815) (suggesting, we might add, mommy issues).

Attempting to classify each person David Hersland comes across while he is alive, the narrator uses winding passageways of language to come back to the same information. Pages filled with repetitive insights take over—about the ways women love, the opinions David's friends and family have about one another, and the feelings of anger that arise between family members. But in revisiting these ideas, the words eventually begin to lose their meaning. For example, we encounter multiple variations of the sentence, "I certainly am certain that I do not want that each one is experiencing each thing differently from the way each one is experiencing each thing" (813).

The wordplay forms paced patterns, rhythmic structures that readers can benefit from reading aloud to experience the full effect of Stein's articulate singsong. Try this one, for example: "**Certainly then each one is himself each one is herself, certainly. Certainly then each one is himself each one is herself certainly then each one is that one in being one being living. Some are certain**
(818) **that each one could be one being certain of something.**" Reading out loud leads to something entirely different from our usual attempts to understand meaning in reading. It reminds us that there is a reason Stein's manner of speaking—the melodic sound of her voice—was so remarked upon in her life. Like her spoken dialogue, her written sentences come in waves, and allowing them to crash on the shore of your mind is the easiest way we have found to interact with them, particularly in this section. We allow ourselves to feel them first and ask questions later. (We should also note that this is the only way we made it through this section while maintaining some sense of reality.)

The narrator's discussion of "angry feeling" seems to go on for days (or about twenty pages), giving us our own ongoing, repeating, angry feelings (832). David comes by this naturally, we understand, because "[e]ach one of the Hersland family could have some angry feeling sometimes in them" (833); "Each one of the Hersland family could have angry feelings in them" (834); "Some are certainly having it again and again from each one being with them in them in family living and for each one are having a certain kind of angry feeling and are certainly having it again and again" (842). These repeating passages turn into "typing" for us; the placement of words of the page, the repeated structures of sentences begin to look arranged. The visuals of the text become more insistent, again more like Stein's later writing. Surrounded by anger in his "younger living," then, David develops the will not to let anger dictate his life. Even when he can't control his anger he becomes upset with himself for being angry.

While the textual fixation on angry feeling remains, we take a couple of side trips, one into how anger intersects with teaching. The narrator persists: "There are different ways of having angry feeling inside each one who is having angry feeling with some one teaching that one" (845). We then explore David's experience with his own teachers. He goes back and forth between trusting their knowledge and not believing them at all. Generally, politeness gets the best of him and he bites his tongue. As the sentences change, David's actions become more of a jumbled mess; sometimes he makes a certain decision only to make a completely different one in the same situation later on (848). This way, David's performed actions aren't clear, and we suspect that the narrator aims to reveal more of his bottom nature through this repetition of his decision-making processes rather than through the decisions themselves. For example, David's unwillingness to learn from governesses in his early life could have entirely disappeared by the time he became a young man, but due to the novel's continuous present, it is not evident at which point these personality changes actually occur in David. Personality changes occur gradually, as the repetition encourages us to see: "Some are changing while they are living in their feeling about being one going on being living about anyone being one going on being living. Some are changing very much in their feeling about this thing." (870)

At the end of the discussion of David's educational challenges, the narrator reappears, interjecting more "I" statements about their own experiences with education: "When I asked something they did not answer that question, certainly they can teach some something, did they or did they not answer the question I asked, certainly not, certainly they did not answer the question I asked, certainly not, certainly they did not answer that question" (847). A few pages later the narrator is apparently reflecting again on how it feels to write this novel: "Certainly it is a trouble to me to be doing this thing" (851). Then they go back to questions asked and answered in what seems like a misplaced rant, even a lover's quarrel, about others asking them for advice: **"You asked me and I told you and you did what I told you and now you are thinking I should have been feeling that you were**
(851) **doing that thing from the feeling you having about that thing."** And then the "I" fades out, as the discussion of advice goes on. A similar personal quarrel reappears on the next page in third person: "Some certainly are liking to be working with sharp knives or sharp scissors, some are not liking to be working with sharp knives or sharp scissors, some have angry feeling when some one has been sharpening the knives or scissors they have been using" (853). This talk of sharpening scissors and knives continues (to our amusement) onto the next page and transitions us back into repetition about angry feeling.

Through the rolling waves of prose in these pages, we glean tidbits of information about David. We learn that, although Martha was the oldest of the Hersland children and David the youngest, David was best at giving advice. And when he gave it, Martha took it: "Certainly she very often listened very much to him" (853). David begins to become "a whole one" as he starts to see his own bottom nature and confronts his anger in the context of his observations about others. "David Hersland was one who almost came to be one certain sometime to be completely understanding being being in men and in women being living. He was one certainly almost and not so very often still quite often coming to be certain of being one completely understanding everything" (857). There are some moments of realization, even conclusion, in his character development, as in repeated sentences that explore his enjoyment of life,

his thinking and conviction: "David Hersland was one certainly in a way not having complete emotion, certainly in a way doing clear thinking, certainly in a way having adequate expression, certainly having very nearly absolute conviction. He had absolute conviction. He had clear thinking, he had adequate expression, he felt inside him complete emotion." Expression, conviction, spirituality, and (859)
idealism are mentioned over and over. David's personality continues to unfold as the narrator relays the qualities of "some," "ones," and "many" back to David. For example: "Many are very logical in being ones being thinking" and "David Hersland was in a way not at all such a one" (861).

At some points in this section, it feels as if Stein opens a floodgate of words on her *TMOA* readers. This paragraph/sentence is illustrative in both its diction and its original layout (which we have maintained with our margins):

> Which way someone is meaning anything, which way some one is
> meaning everything, how some one is meaning what that one is saying,
> meaning feeling, thinking and being certain, what that one is doing,
> feeling, thinking and of what that one is certain, how that one is going
> on meaning something, meaning anything, meaning everything, which
> way that one is going on meaning what that one is saying, feeling, think-
> ing, doing, and what connection in that one between living in that one
> and being in that one, how that one is liking is not liking what that one
> means to say to any one knowing that one, how that one is liking is not lik-
> ing what that one is not meaning to some one, to any one, how anything
> coming into that one come out of that one, how some things coming into
> that one hardly are coming out of that one, how much the things coming
> out of that one are different from the things going into that one, how quick-
> ly and how slowly, how completely, how gradually, how intermittently,
> how noisily, how silently, how happily, how drearily, how difficultly, how
> gaily, how complicatedly, how simply, how joyously, how boisterously,
> how despondingly, how fragmentarily, how delicately, how roughly, how
> excitedly, how energetically, how persistently, how repeatedly, how repeat-
> ingly, how drily, how startlingly, how funnily, how certainly, how
> hesitatingly, anything is coming out of that one, what is being in each

one and how anything comes into that one and comes out of that one makes of each one one meaning something and feeling, telling, thinking,
(863-4) being certain and being living.

Even when we sense we're wading in over our heads, passages like this leap from the page and make it clear that there is artistry and arrangement here, purpose and technique.

Like the personality traits surrounding most "ones," a contradictory flow of personality traits engulfs David through this section, confusing us, confusing him: "In a way David Hersland did know very well what kind he was of ones experiencing, of ones expressing, in a way he never came to be completely certain that he was not perhaps another kind of a one experiencing, another kind of one expressing" (864). Sometimes David "is such a one" and sometimes he is not. If we think about each of these personality traits occurring at different times in David's life (since the text itself jumps through tense and time), it would follow that David was, at some point, not interested in understanding and learning about others, "feeling very strongly about something," or frequently experiencing anger (868). He could, "in a way," be both "not completely interested in this thing" and "almost completely interested in this thing" (869). If we think about David not as contradictory, but as a human being developing over time, then sentences in this section can be located in different places through his life, becoming not contradictory but illuminating and atemporal. In this way, Stein can capture ever-changing and developing human beings without being tied to any particular time in their lives, to any of their shifting opinions or fluid identities. In doing this, she expressly aims to locate essences, essential beings in them, how they are "of a kind in men and women" (872).

This search for David's being culminates in his "not any longer" being, in pages full of reactions to his death from the people who knew him in life. "Some one was very indignant that he had come to be a dead one and almost went out to where he was not any longer living to complain to some one about this thing (874). Another was "tenderly completely a sad one and then always was about this thing about David Hersland being a dead one" (873-4). These continue on and off through the remainder of the David section, as we revisit his death repeatedly. He is "in a way . . . one having been living in being living" (874). He continues to be alive in the text and through these responses among the living. And that's good, because he doesn't live on through children, as many choose to do. David wasn't particularly fascinated with babies and cared neither about having one nor being one (874).

As we think about babies and muse about young people and their reactions to death, verb tenses connected to our examination of "ones" or "some" shift more quickly than readers might consciously notice. "Is," "are," and "have been" appear one after the other, highlighting the narrative's preoccupation with temporality. "Remembering," "remembered," and "remember" show up often, as the prospect of dying and being forgotten, hard as it is to grasp, haunts this section. **"Certainly to very many being living when they are being young ones being a dead one is a thing that is a thing a little terrifying, not very exciting, quite interesting, not happening, certainly not happening."** (878)

There follows a funny, repeated section about jumping. The narrator correlates being young with the act of "completely jumping": "Certainly very many when they are being young ones are ones then talking then and jumping then and certainly some of such of them are ones certainly feeling themselves being completely then ones talking, ones jumping" (879-80). David "was one of such of" these jumping young ones. These riffs invite us to think of being young and alive and excited to take on new opportunities. We had flashes of jumping for joy. And this is how the twists of Stein's language work. Distinctive word choices and changing combinations call our attention to feelings and themes. For example, these variations of a sentence opener appear in one paragraph: "To some certainly not anyone is ever a young one"; "To some everyone is sometimes a young one"; and "To some certainly not anyone is ever a young one" (881).

These pages, though they often leave us lost in language, emphasize that David was really good at being "a young one," at doing all the things involved in "being living." David was also highly skilled at "jumping" which is repeated so often there is no way to miss it. The guy could jump.

Whether or not people are truly living their lives to the fullest seems to be the primary concern here.

Whether or not some people are doing more than "just breathing" while they are living, we learn that even "David Hersland was sometimes not liking being one going on being living, he certainly was sometimes not liking being one going on being living, he certainly was one sometimes, almost always liking being one going on being living then (885). This cues the novel's shift to a focus on pure rhythm of language. One paragraph begins:

> One is doing something and then doing that thing again and then doing another thing and then doing that thing again and then doing the one thing and then the other thing and that one certainly would be doing some other thing and doing that thing again and would be then doing another thing and would be doing that thing again and would then be doing the one thing and then would be doing the other if that one were not doing the things that
> (886) one is doing in being one being living.

The novel goes on in a similar way for several pages where the words "certainly," "again," "another thing," "being," and "living" stand out. The rhythm captures us again a few pages later in repetitions about "being a young one": "When one is a young one one is a young one. Certainly when one is a young one one is then a young one" and so on (889). We find ourselves holding onto these moments of clarity like life preservers, even as we respond to the ebbs and flows of Steinian language around us.

And so we beat on, moving toward understanding of human motivation and its justifications—youth, fear, necessity. David, again, shares the narrator's fascination with understanding and explanation, why people do what they do. Like the narrator (and like Stein), "He was one listening and talking and asking and answering" (900). He needed "to be realising the different ways any one can be thinking, feeling, doing at different times in being living, in being a young one, an older one, a middle aged one, an older one, an old one, a very old one" (901). And David struggles on, taking up the narrator's task—sometimes knowing, sometimes feeling, sometimes understanding those around him.

Pages 905–998 | This break in the David Hersland section does not signal any change in form or content. As we continue our pursuit of words and of David's character, "pleased" joins "certainly" and "living" in the rings of repetition. His quest for "knowing" and "understanding" remain central, and "some" and "ones" still claim our attention in the gradual telling of how people get to know David and interact with him throughout his life. The words on the page become increasingly striking, almost mechanized in the gears and cogs of their arrangement.

We begin with past tense verbs for David, "when he was living," and remain in the past for several pages. Meanwhile, "some one" appears in present tense: "Some one understanding some one is telling that one" (909), in another example of how tenses change, slowly or rapidly, back and forth in this novel. Here "was" and "were" are replaced with "are" and "is," in some cases within the same few sentences.

Now narrating in third-person, the text reaffirms David's place in the world as "the son born of his mother Fanny Hersland after Martha Hersland, Alfred Hersland and the two who did not come to be ones going on being living were born out of her" (911). But then emphasizes quickly that "He was different, quite different from his mother and his father and his sister and his brother" (911). We recall that he was once "a young one" and that "Surely David Hersland said some things and did some things that some said he said and some said he did" (912). So here, at the beginning of the final section of this novel devoted to the Hersland children, the text seems intent on thwarting any expectations of plot. David is unique, but he is also every man, "some one." We need to know that "Each one in being living is saying things, is doing things. David Hersland in being living was doing things, was saying things." (914)

A page full of some one "wondering" and "certainly" being "astonished" follows, after which we home in again on David, now in present tense, thinking, feeling, wanting. In these pages, words leap out as they are repeated and re-arranged. Three short paragraphs call our attention to versions of this sentence: "Some are [not] liking someone and are telling about that thing" (918). Then several longer paragraphs repeat and expand on this theme, on liking, knowing, needing.

As we struggle to make meaning of these almost mechanical reitera-
(922) tions, a vivid character insight appears: **"Some one sometimes ran after him."** This some one "sometimes ran after David Hersland when he was walking and that one ran quite breathless then said to him, how are you, and then that one did not really have anything to say to him." But this one is never gendered. In fact, the text seems to make a point of avoiding pronouns, noting that "such a one" was, to David, "a silly one." When they got to David, this one was tired, or breathless, or wordless; they shook hands and said "how are you," then "certainly had not anything to say to him" (923).

But what is striking to us is how the text immediately transitions, in the next paragraph, to how David "was one certainly in a way needing to be certain that every woman was in a way a beautiful thing. Certainly not any woman was in a way a beautiful thing to him" (923). We assume that the text alludes to David's sexuality in this way, leading us to wonder whether David is to be construed as queer. He was, we learn, "needing to be completely wanting to be seeing some one. Certainly some one sometimes ran after him," that someone who has no identifiable gender (923). What is clear (certainly) is that Stein was revolutionary in her avoidance of pronouns, in her embracing of identities, sexualities and relationships that couldn't be contained in a heteronormative system.

As David's death (and the end of the novel) nears, we start to see more references to dying. Various versions of a few sentences weave through the next few pages: "Certainly very many are being living" (925) and "Certainly very many are being living, very many are dying, very many are commencing existing" (926), sometimes bringing it home to "David Hersland was being existing, certainly David Hersland was dying, certainly David Hersland was commencing existing" (926). Some are sad about that, and the text ruminates on the idea in a few simple sentences, shifting and circling around it. "Some are sad enough, certainly they are sad enough. Some are not sad enough, certainly they are not sad enough" (926). Then

"Some are sad enough. Some are not sad enough" (927). And, again, back to David, who "was not a sad one, he was a sad one" (928). The narrator's presence has faded here, their own emotion unacknowledged.

We reflect, again, on the process of aging, how "little by little they are not so young those being young" (929). Here the tenses shift and "little by little" becomes "quickly" one is not so young, and, before the paragraph is over, "One is then still young" (929). Now being young is connected not with jumping but with being tossed and "tossing himself" (929). We go back, then, to David, who doesn't realize how constant change is until he is well into his middle living. The idea that people change shocks him because he is unaware of how much he himself is changing:

> One is thinking and he is thinking quite the same thing he has been thinking since he commenced thinking and always and always it is a little older, a little different and a little different and it is a very pleasant thing to some to see in any one, to see in themselves little growing difference in them and then it is like a map of anything, one is finding that the real thing is like the description. (930)

If there is anything we learn from this section it is that young, middle aged, and old people all have different ways of doing the same thing over and over again. We see this in David as we let his life pass before our eyes for a few pages. While he develops over time, he also remains the same in many ways. He is troubled, he writes things down, he did "some things very well" (935), he "decided some things," he "sometimes smelled something then remembered something" (938), he knows things, he thinks things, he "was clearly feeling what he was feeling" (942), he "was a noisy one" (945), he was "being living every day" (951), until he wasn't. "In a way it is a gentle thing to be one being not any longer living," the narrator notes, impersonally (945).

Even after pages of reflecting on and summing up David's life, the shift from living to dead seems abrupt, occurring as it does in clear, simple sentences: "He was being living every day all of his being living. He was dead when he was at the ending of the beginning of being in middle living. He was dead by then. He was dead and buried by then" (952). But just in case anyone missed it, the text emphasizes and reemphasizes how alive David had been, how much he "was being living every day. He was knowing every day that he was being living that day" (952):

> David Hersland lived as long as he was living and he certainly sometimes was quite certain that he needed to be completely expressing the feeling that certainly there was not any succeeding in living, that certainly it was enough not to have been ever living, that it would have been enough to have not been one coming to be living, that having been living, being living had
> (954) not in any way any meaning.

It's comforting to know that even the very alive, jumping David has occasional trouble with the concept of living. Apparently, sometimes even he thinks, "I think I've had enough of this."

In this final revisiting of David's life, focused less on his particularity and more on his universal humanity, it's surprising when the text revisits his romantic life, sketching in more specific detail. We learn that "Someone was almost coming to be loving him" (956). Up until this point, David's love life has been elusive, and his sexuality even more so. David clearly has a human need for connection: "Sometimes he was with one, sometimes he was with two, sometimes he was with three, sometimes he was with more than three" (942). We learn that: "He was sometimes wanting to be needing another one. He was sometimes needing another one. He was often enough wanting to be needing another one. He was sometimes almost needing another
(958) one." We get the sense that David hid himself in plain sight, surrounded by friends, rather than discuss his feelings of loneliness and his desire for "another one."

When he does eventually gather the courage to express love for someone, this love of his is discussed using feminine pronouns, as in "he was loving her." The narrator elaborates: "He was loving one then and he was in a way telling this thing, telling it to her and others were knowing it then and
(961) in a way it was not interesting to her and he was not really telling it to her then."
Here, at the end of his life, David seems interested in loving another person.

"Each one is one," the narrator asserts, simply (961). David, having discovered this truth, is then "giving advice" to people about it. Or not. "He was not in any way wanting to give advice" (963). He was knowing; he was interested; he wanted to both understand people and being understood in return. "He was one with some of them, in being one of them, in being one understanding something, in being one going to be using understanding something to understanding everything" (964). The next few pages suggest that David's desire to be "one of them" is innate, as the desire to belong resides in most of us. When we return one more time to review David's life, the contradiction continues. David is "quietly being one being living" (972). No wait, "David Hersland was not quite quietly enough being one being living. That was certain" (974). How to sum up a life, then, when different people will tell different stories about anyone?

A nice folding in of connections follows when David "came to know almost any one who knew Julia Hersland. He came to know very many who were knowing Alfred Hersland. He came to know every one whom George Dehning was knowing" (975). David seems particularly connected to Julia, his brother's ex-wife. He "was completely convincing" to her as he considered whether "thinking is existing" (979). And starting here, the concrete exploration of David as an individual is underlined with a pattern of uncharacteristically short paragraphs that begin, relentlessly, with David. Each paragraph opens with: "He was," "He was not," or "David Hersland was." In fact, from page 972 to 986, every paragraph but four, with generally five or six paragraphs to a page, begins similarly, with David. Each is concerned with David's understanding, his thinking and telling, his doing and working, his needing and succeeding, his being and his living.

Again, the text leaves us with the impression that David really wants to become a person who understands everything and is fully aware of his own life, before his death. It suggests that his ultimate goal is to realize his entire self, almost as if he is reaching for some form of enlightenment, as in this (typical) paragraph:

> He was often quite alone with being one being living, and working, clearly

> working to be completely understanding this thing. He was often almost quite alone and he was not suffering, not at all suffering. He was clearly working, he was working and clearly working and he was clearly thinking and he was almost clearly feeling. He was almost completely clearly expressing that he was clearly working. He was clearly expressing that he was
> (983) clearly thinking.

The attempt to realize David's character—for himself, the novelist, and the reader—is constant and repetitive, but the repetition seems more certain and powerful here, perhaps because of the shorter sentences and paragraphs. "He was not one really needing something. He was one being interesting. He was one knowing that he was keeping an open mind. He was doing something of this thing, he was keeping an open mind" (987).

The narrative also occasionally drops tidbits of information about the people in David's life, as when it revisits his family, particularly Alfred and Julia (never Martha), and then extends into his later connections with the Dehning family. At one point, we zoom out to see David as the Dehnings see him: "Each one of the Dehning family came to tell him something of that one knowing him . . . Mr. Dehning came to know him and told him of this thing of knowing him. He told him that he liked it well enough knowing him, that he liked it very well knowing him and that he David Hersland was a man to understand something of such a thing of Mr. Dehning knowing him" (988). This process repeats with Mrs. Dehning and then Julia, George and Hortense.

Following this final review, we near the end of David's section and, again, the end of his life. "He had come to quite completely not eating anything but one thing. He was strong then, he was strong in completely clearly thinking then . . . He was living then in being living. He was then not going on being living" (992). Finally, as the chapter ends, David "had come to be a dead one and he was then at the ending of beginning living. He had come to be a dead one and some then were knowing that thing knowing then that he was not any longer being living. Some were then knowing that he was
(995) a dead one.

The tense switches when discussing David as the narrator favors "had been" and "had come to be," and David shifts subtly from subject to object: "Some knew he was a dead one" (996). In the final paragraph of the David section, he is dead and buried, and these "some" are surprised, indignant, wondering, interested remembering, certain and uncertain about David. How memorable was this man? This narrative? The text equivocates, ending vaguely: "Any one could be one not very constantly remembering his being a dead one, his having been a living one. Any one could remember this thing, his having been a dead one, his having been a living one." (998)

Part Four

[History of a Family's Progress]

Pages 1002–1022 | Though Stein's first full draft of this novel ends with David "having been a dead one," the final handwritten text adds this final, universalizing section. Though there is a page break between the end of David's section and the "History of a Family's Progress," the sentences seem to flow uninterrupted from David's final "having been a dead one, his having been a living one" to the opening of this last chapter: "Any one has come to be a dead one" (1002). But there is, in fact, a huge shift here. The novel now leaves behind first person altogether; the narrator's voice has long been silent. It leaves behind specifics of character; no Herslands or Dehnings remain to attend to. Using the now familiar repetitive style, it moves into collective conclusions about all of the people ever living, and further, all of the people who have already or will in the future, come to die.

From the introductory paragraph to the conclusion seventeen pages later, the narrative riffs on universals: we are living, then we are dead. Living or dead. These are our only options, and one flows into the other: **"Any one has come to be a dead one. Any one has not come to be such a one to be a dead one. Many who are living have not come yet to be a dead one. Many who were living have come to be a dead one. Any one has come not to be dead one. Any one has come to be a dead one."** Nobody is immune to death at any age, we (1002) learn over and over. "Any old ones come to be dead. Any one coming to be an old enough one comes to be a dead one. Old ones come to be dead ones. Any one not coming to be a dead one before coming to be an old one comes to be an old one and comes then to be a dead one as any old one comes to be a dead one (1020). The transition from "some" to "any one" in the face of death is haunting and intriguing, because it is the one common experience that we will all, without a doubt, share.

As if to mediate the devastation of death, the novel returns to types and to "family living," to some revisiting of how we live when we live. We fall into familiar classifying of "kinds of ones," of men and women who are still alive, their hopes and dreams still achievable. But we are never allowed to forget that human potential is quickly swallowed up by the abruptness of our collective death. The fact that all of us will die is drilled relentless throughout the final section. In fact, our now detached third-person narrator, having guided us through elaborations of their own sorrows, deep frustrations, regrets, achievements, and glee, points out, austerely, in the middle of this section, that, "Some one was standing and doing something" (1014).

That sentence effectively represents the tone of this text, with various "some ones," "any ones," "old ones" vaguely (hopelessly?) striving for certainty and understanding. They are being and doing, needing, and remembering. They organize into families where "any one can be married in them and some in them are not married and some in them are married and any one of them almost any one of them can have some children and some of them have some children and some of them do not have children and some of them do something, do anything again" (1008). We learn that families all contain the living and dead, the young and the old, and eventually the possibility of family extinction arises. The narrator, in their repetitive, roundabout way, poses the question most people avoid: What happens when nobody is left to remember us?

Family living is significant, then, because where there is a family there are people who remain to remember, to share traditions, generational knowledge, language, and grandma's favorite recipes—to essentially keep the essence of a family alive. The storyteller, the one who is "hearing everything" then "saying something" keeps the family "being living" (1010):

> Any one being one being in any family living is being one having been saying something. Any one being living is one having been saying something Any one being in any family living is one having been saying something again. Any one being living is one having been saying something again. Any one being in any family living is one saying something again. Any one being in any family living is one saying something and saying anything again. Any one being living is one saying something again. Any one being living is one saying anything and saying anything again. [Spacing and punctuation in the original.] (1011)

This becomes the focus of the final pages, as we move toward the ultimate realization that "Any family living can be one being existing and some can remember something of some such thing." (1022)

And that's all, folks. The vagueness of memory meets the inevitability of death with the possibility that "Very many are remembering this thing are remembering that family living can go on existing" (1022). This is the story of a decent family's progress, from specificity of experience, collections of histories, connections, and types, to a misty fading from being living to coming to be a dead one, with no promise of continuity, only the possibility that someone will remember and tell the story.

And they may have just done that.

Bibliography of Significant Sources on *TMOA*

* American Literature Collection, Beinecke Rare Book and Manuscript Library, Yale University. "Gertrude Stein and Alice B. Toklas Papers." (n.d.).
* Benstock, Sheri. *Women of the Left Bank*. University of Texas Press, 1987.
* Boyd, Janet and Sharon J. Kirsch. *Primary Stein: Returning to the Writing of Gertrude Stein*. New York: Lexington Books, 2014. Print.
* Clement, Tanya E. "The Makings of Digital Modernism: Rereading Gertrude Stein's 'the Making of Americans' and Poetry by Elsa Von Freytag-Loringhoven." University of Maryland, College Park, 2009
* Cody, Morrill and Hugh Ford. *The Women of Montparnasse: The Americans in Paris*. Cranbury, NJ: Cornwall, 1984.
* Craig, Gavin. "*The Making of Americans*: Language, Plot and Being Mistaken." Michigan State University, December 2010. Dissertation.
* DuPlessis, Rachel Blau. "Woofenstein, the Sequel" in *Primary Stein: Returning to the Writing of Gertrude Stein*, Janet Boyd and Sharon J. Kirsch, eds. New York: Lexington Books, 2014. 37-56. Print
* Gilbert, Sandra and Susan Gubar. *No Man's Land: The Place of the Woman Writer in the Twentieth Century*. New Haven: Yale UP, 1987, 1989, 1996. Print.

* Hoffman, Michael J. *The Development of Abstractionism in the Writings of Gertrude Stein*. University of Pennsylvania Press, 2016.
* Kaufmann, Michael. "Gertrude Stein's *The Making of Americans*: Repetition and the Emergence of Modernism (review)." *American Literature*, vol. 71 no. 4, 1999, pp. 807-808. *Project MUSE*
* Kern, Stephen. *The Modernist Novel: A Critical Introduction*. Cambridge: Cambridge UP, 2011. Print.
* Lorange, Astrid. *How Reading is Written, a Brief Index to Gertrude Stein*. Wesleyan University Press, December 2014.
* Loth, Valérie. *Matisse, Cezanne, Picasso: L'aventure Des Stein*. Exhibition Catalogue (Album de L'Exposition) Paris: Grand Palais, Galeries nationales, 2011.
* Mellow, James R. *Charmed Circle: Gertrude Stein and Company*. Boston: Houghton Mifflin, 1974. Print.
* McCallum, E.L. *Unmaking the Making of Americans : Toward an Aesthetic Ontology*. State University of New York Press, 2018.
* Moore, George. *Repetition and the Emergence of Modernism*. Peter Lang, 1998.
* Neuman, S.C, and Ira Bruce Nadel. *Gertrude Stein and the Making of Literature*. Northeastern University Press, 1988.
* Rainey, Lawrence S. "The Making of Americans (Review)." *Modernism/Modernity* (1997): 222-224
* Ruddick, Lisa. *Gertrude Stein: Body, Text, Gnosis*. Cornell University Press, 1990.
* Solomon, Jeff. *So Famous and So Gay: The Fabulous Potency of Truman Capote and Gertrude Stein*. Minneapolis MN: U of MN Press, 2017. Print.
* Stein, Gertrude. *The Making of Americans*. London: Dalkey Archive, 1995 (from the 1925 Contact Edition). Print.
* _____ and Sherwood Anderson. *Geography and Plays*. Boston: The Four Seas Company, 1922.

ONLINE AT GOOGLEBOOKS.COM.

* _____and Ulla E. Dydo. *A Stein Reader*. Northwestern University Press, 1993.
* Wagner-Martin, Linda. *Favored Strangers: Gertrude Stein and Her Family*. New Brunswick, NJ: Rutgers \ UP, 1995. Print.
* Welch, Lew. *How I Read Gertrude Stein*. Grey Fox Press, 2001.

Acknowledgements

BOTH OF US want to thank the members of the Gertrude Stein Senior Seminar, Fall 2016, who were the original Team Gertrude. We couldn't have done this without you: Maia Labrie, Ash Larson, Shoua Yang, Lauren Crepeau, Ann Blatzheim, honorary Gertrude student, Annie Byrne, and our enthusiastic and supportive collaborator Emma Hargreaves. Here's the guide we all wanted.

We also want to thank St. Catherine University and the Summer Undergraduate Collaborative Research Program that jumpstarted our work in 2017, as well as the Carondelet Scholars research fund that kept it going, and the internal research grant that supported our unforgettable sojourn at the Beinecke Library in January 2018. We want to honor the generosity of the Gertrude Stein Society; they included three of us on a panel at the American Literature Association Conference in 2018, expressed encouraging enthusiasm for our work, and sent us off with renewed commitment to this project. Thank you again, Ellen McCallum, Amy Robbins, and John Varghese, teachers and mentors all. And thanks to J&S Bean Factory for the Wi-Fi, coffee and hospitality. This is what we were doing with that big book.

Cecilia would like to thank Janie for saying "yes"—yes to reading a really big novel in the first place, yes to writing a book about how to read it. I have loved working side-by-side with you and matching my enthusiasm to yours. Thanks, as always, to my mom, Grace Konchar, who in every way that matters made me what I am—a book lover, a questioner, a writer. I honor my dad who believed I could do hard things, from playing the violin to going to college. And, finally, thanks to Cubs, T. D., Daley, and Max, my solid support system and my favorite readers.

Janie would like to thank Cecilia for cheerfully, yet determinedly, charging into our senior seminar with a novel that would change my life for years to come (seriously, years). And thank you to my wife, Carly, who has lovingly and (mostly) patiently, allowed me to recite lines from *The Making of Americans* to her for the past two years and then some. My friends (Laura, MB, Rhys, Sylvia, Ash, Mel, Boey) and sister, Jenna, who showed up for countless dinners, brought me wine, and listened when I needed to borrow an ear (or some editing expertise) for Gertrude Related Reasons. Shout out to you too, Dad. You always invest in me with your emotions, with your time, with your thoughtful discussions. And Bonnie, a true supporter, supermom and powerhouse, where would I be without you? Let's not find out. But most of all, a big thanks to Gertrude Stein, Lesbian icon, total inspiration, and invaluable model of human growth and immense strength of character.

BIOGRAPHICAL INFORMATION

Cecilia Konchar Farr is Dean of the College of Liberal and Creative Arts at West Liberty State University in West Virginia where, in addition to her work as dean, she teaches, researches, and writes about higher education, popular literature and the history of the novel. She is author of The Ulysses Delusion: Rethinking Standards of Literary Merit and Reading Oprah: How Oprah's Book Club Changes the Way America Reads, and editor of several essay collections. An English professor, feminist theorist, and faculty advocate, she lives in Pittsburgh, just across the river from Gertrude Stein's first home.

Janie Sisson is a writer, researcher, community organizer, and activist from San Bernardino, California. She holds an MA in applied gender and cultural studies from Claremont Graduate University. In her spare time, you'll find her reading a book in the sun, camping and exploring in the mountains with her family, or trying out new recipes for friends. She currently lives in northern Colorado with her wife and their rescue dog, Clover.

www.ingramcontent.com/pod-product-compliance
Lightning Source LLC
Jackson TN
JSHW070732071125
93598JS00001B/1

* 9 7 8 1 6 2 8 9 7 4 5 8 4 *